December 25, 2002

Merry Christmas Mom!

I Love you very much

Love Always,

Cynthia

The
Stonewall Kitchen
Cookbook

WM

WILLIAM MORROW
75 YEARS OF PUBLISHING
An Imprint of HarperCollins*Publishers*

The Stonewall Kitchen Cookbook

favorite pantry recipes

JONATHAN KING & JIM STOTT

HarperCollins books may be purchased for educational, business, or sales promotional use. For information please write: Special Markets Department, HarperCollins Publishers Inc., 10 East 53rd Street, New York, NY 10022.

FIRST EDITION

Designed by Leah Carlson-Stanisic

Food photographs by Quentin Bacon
Scenic photographs by Jim Stott except for pages x, xi, 27, 49, 84, 107–108, 125

Table linens courtesy Just Linens Ltd., 770 Lexington Avenue, New York, NY 10021.

Printed on acid-free paper

Library of Congress Cataloging-in-Publication Data
King, Jonathan.
     The Stonewall Kitchen cookbook : favorite pantry recipes / by Jonathan King and Jim Stott — 1st ed.
        p. cm
     Includes index.
     ISBN 0-06-019783-8
     1. Condiments. I. Stott, Jim. II. Stonewall Kitchen (Store) III. Title.

TX819.A1.K55 2001
641.6'382—dc21

                                                                                            00–050078

01 02 03 04 05 / RRD 10 9 8 7 6 5 4 3 2 1

*To Donna King, my mother, whom I thank every day for buying me
my first Easy Bake Oven and fostering my passion. I am glad that you were here long
enough to see the beginnings of our success. I miss you and wish you were
here to share all this with us. Thanks, mom.*

—JONATHAN KING

*To Pearl Oxner, my late grandmother, who at age ninety-six worked
tirelessly for us at the farmer's market, never complained, and never got paid. Thanks, Nannie.
And to Tramp, who begged for a taste of every pot of jam and was
with me faithfully for almost twenty years.*

—JIM STOTT

Acknowledgments

From our first sales in 1991 at a local farmer's market to the realization of this cookbook, Stonewall Kitchen's success has been just an incredible dream come true for both of us. Through the efforts of many people throughout the years, we have truly experienced the bountiful goodness of our simple garden's treasures and are now fortunate to be able to share our recipes around the world.

The work of creating this book has been an exciting pleasure and we have many thanks to extend.

To Harriet Bell, our friend and editor, for her vision, education, and professional guidance through the world of publishing and for many incredible memories of wonderful meals and fun along the way. To the William Morrow associates, Kate Stark, marketing director; Carrie Weinberg, director of publicity; Roberto de Vicq de Cumptich, art director; Leah Carlson-Stanisic, design manager; Karen Lumley, senior production manager; and Ann Cahn, senior production editor, whose talents are enormous.

To Bruce Weinstein for his invaluable assistance, talents, and friendship.

To Quentin Bacon and his assistant, Tina Rupp, for images that are beautiful representations of our culinary art.

To our loyal customers who have followed us through these many years, from the farmer's market to "the barn," to our beautiful new facility, your faithful, continued patronage has been the motivation for us to do the best we can, because we know that's what you've grown to expect and what we truly want to share.

To both of our families, who have supported us in many ways over the years, both with their hard work and dollars (thanks, Peg) when we needed them. We love you all.

And finally to the staff at Stonewall Kitchen, part of our family, our deepest gratitude for supporting our dream, working hard, and for sharing lots of laughs with us along the way. Without each one of you, Stonewall Kitchen would still be just a dream. Thank you, sincerely.

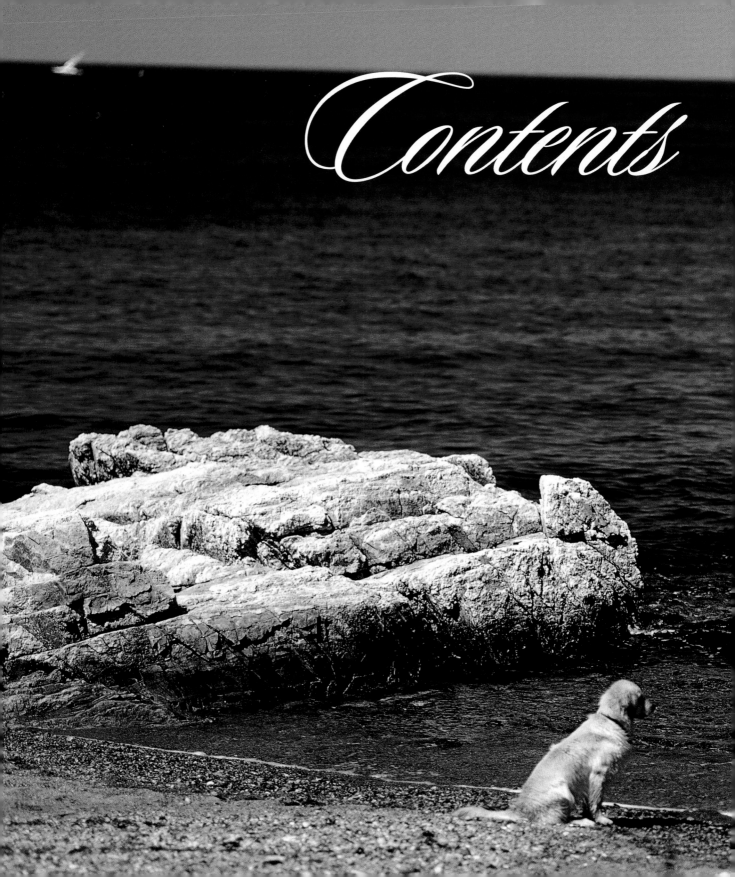

Contents

ACKNOWLEDGMENTS   IX

INTRODUCTION   1

Breakfast
5

Soups and Sandwiches
29

Appetizers
45

Pastas and Salads
61

Seafood
77

Meat
97

Vegetables and Sides
115

Desserts
129

Drinks
149

Stonewall Kitchen Products
155

Stonewall Kitchen Store Guide
157

INDEX   158

Introduction

By late September in 1994, the blueberry barrens across Maine had turned burnt red. Frost covered the ground and our breath froze in the chilly air as we loaded the truck on the last Saturday morning of the month. We had a stall at the farmer's market in Portsmouth, New Hampshire, where we sold our preserves. When we drove there that day, we knew that it would be our last season at the market. Our first Stonewall Kitchen store was under construction.

The sun had barely warmed the air when we pulled up to the market at 6:00 A.M. As always, our customers were waiting in line, warming their hands on hot cups of cider and cocoa. They waited for us to open our boxes, eager to see what new jam, relish, or chutney we had developed that week. There was always something new. Each week, as the crowds cleared out in the late afternoon, we bartered with the farmers, exchanging preserves for their produce. Those fruits and vegetables would be what we preserved and sold the following week.

When summer fruit was on hand, we'd make jam, sometimes simply capturing the intense flavor of blueberries, at other times combining ingredients like raspberries, peaches, and a touch of Champagne for a sophisticated taste. When beans or cucumbers were picked, we pickled them. And when onions and garlic were all the farmers had to barter, we experimented and created our Roasted Garlic & Onion Jam. Within a few years this unusual combination would win us awards.

Since we used what was readily available, our menu changed every week, something our customers came to expect. They too shared our passion for fresh and innovative flavors. On that market day in 1994, we knew that we would miss the friends who worked by our sides, but we looked forward to greeting our loyal customers year-round at our first Stonewall Kitchen store that winter.

We've often been asked why we called our company Stonewall Kitchen. Drive through Maine and you'll see miles of old stone walls lining family farms—bright red barns against deep blue skies and bales of hay drying in the sun. There was a beautiful wall outside our first kitchen. Both handcrafted and permanent, it was the perfect symbol for our growing company. So we wrote Stonewall Kitchen on each label.

Today, we still use only the best quality ingredients in our products. Our Red Pepper Jelly, for example, is made only in the late fall, when red peppers are harvested. And our Maine Blueberry Jam offers the taste of a Maine summer in every jar. (And it's still our handwriting on the labels.) Note that ingredients in capitals refer to our products.

"WHAT CAN I DO WITH IT?"

That's the question our customers often ask. So we've put together this collection of recipes to show just how easy it is to make all sorts of food taste better, quickly and easily, with our condiments and preserves.

Of course, our innovative condiments can be used to spark up a simple sandwich, but there are so many other ways you can use our products to bring flavor and exciting new tastes to every-day meals.

Flavored mustards perk up the simplest of dishes, like mashed potatoes and grilled cheese sandwiches. But they're also perfect with more sophisticated fare, such as rack of lamb. Chutneys can be mixed into vegetable salads or served in sandwiches instead of mayonnaise or ketchup. And jams have a much bigger role than just a toast-topping at breakfast. They can be used in appetizers, entrées, and desserts. We've even used jam for a pie filling when fresh berries weren't available.

Sure, our parents knew the convenience of cooking with condiments. It's not a new secret. But the condiments in our contemporary pantry are more flavorful, more sophisticated.

Each of these recipes calls for one Stonewall Kitchen product that makes the dish unique. If you don't have our products on hand, don't worry—you'll find alternatives listed in the recipe, so you can always enjoy some of our favorite food. But getting our products is easy. They're available in many gourmet shops, through our catalogue and website and in our Stonewall Kitchen stores.

We've built each of those stores with an open kitchen. There, we continue to make these very recipes, as well as the new recipes that we're developing all the time. So, when customers ask "What can I do with it?," we not only have an answer but we have something good for them to taste.

Breakfast

Maine has rolling hills, forested mountains, beautiful lakes, and pristine mill ponds. But the most beautiful scene of all is the sun rising over the Atlantic as the lobster boats head out to haul up their traps. On the weekends, we often invite guests to breakfast so they can enjoy this view with us. Before we eat, we all marvel at this sight as we walk with our two Golden Retrievers on Ogunquit's Marginal Way, the one-mile hilltop path along the ocean.

Breakfast is a great time for entertaining. Everyone shows up with a clear mind and a rested body. We always cook large breakfasts because everyone's guaranteed to be hungry.

If you have time, bake a batch of Jam Muffins, stuff some French Toast, or make a platter of sweet, rich Baked Apples. For a leisurely winter brunch, Pumpkin-Cranberry Spice Bread will fill your house with an inviting aroma as it bakes. For special occasions, try Lobster Eggs Benedict and Spicy Maine Home Fries. When time is short, try make-ahead Maine-style Maple-Blueberry Granola. Fried Eggs with Curry-Browned Butter and Chutney also make a quick and satisfying dish. All of these breakfast dishes offer you the true essence of Maine.

Maple-Blueberry Granola

Packaged granolas are often loaded with fat and sugar. Our version is lower in fat and slightly sweetened. It's a real time-saver if you make it ahead, especially in double batches, as we often do. We use maple and blueberry syrups from our pantry—two authentic tastes of Maine. If you don't have blueberry syrup, use all maple instead—the dried blueberries will carry the blueberry flavor on their own. Serve this granola with milk or plain yogurt for a hearty breakfast.

Preheat the oven to 300°F.

Combine the oats, coconut, sunflower seeds, almonds, wheat germ, brown sugar, and cinnamon in a large mixing bowl and toss until well combined.

Combine the maple syrup, blueberry syrup, oil, honey, and vanilla in a small mixing bowl and stir until well blended. Pour over the oat mixture and toss, using two large wooden spoons, until the dry ingredients have absorbed all the liquid.

Spread the mixture onto two 11 x 17-inch baking sheets. (If you have only one large baking sheet, bake the granola in two batches.) Bake for 30 minutes, stirring the granola and reversing the baking sheets, top to bottom, every 5 to 10 minutes.

Remove the baking sheets from the oven and sprinkle ½ cup of the blueberries over each sheet. Set the sheets on racks and cool the granola completely, stirring once or twice. Store the granola in an airtight container at room temperature for up to 6 weeks.

3½ cups rolled oats

1½ cups unsweetened shredded coconut

½ cup unsalted sunflower seeds

½ cup whole, raw almonds (unblanched)

½ cup wheat germ

¼ cup packed light brown sugar

2 teaspoons ground cinnamon

½ cup Maine Maple Syrup

¼ cup Wild Maine Blueberry Syrup or maple syrup

½ cup canola oil

2 tablespoons honey

2 teaspoons vanilla extract

1 cup dried blueberries (or dark raisins)

MAKES ABOUT 8 CUPS

Baked Apples

By autumn's first cold snap, the roadside stands in Maine are bursting with red, green, and yellow apples. With so many apples, we like to whip up a batch of these baked apples for brunch, stuffed with nuts and sugar, then basted with our Apple Butter Syrup. While they bake, the syrup reduces with the apples' natural juices to create a golden sauce. Although they should be served warm, you can bake them the night before, then reheat them, covered, in a 375°F oven for about 10 minutes before serving. Of course, you can also do as our mothers did and serve them for dessert, with a big scoop of butter pecan or vanilla ice cream.

Preheat the oven to 375°F.

Core 1 apple using the smaller scoop of a melon baller: Start at the stem, scooping down into the apple and rotating the melon baller as you go; stop before you break through the bottom of the apple. Then use the melon baller to enlarge the cavity inside the apple, creating a hollow slightly larger than a walnut. Using a vegetable peeler, peel 6 to 8 evenly spaced vertical strips of skin from the apple, creating a striped effect. Immediately rub the outside of the apple with 1 of the lemon halves, squeeze a few drops of lemon juice into the cavity, and rub the inside of the apple with your finger to make sure the walls of the cavity are moistened with lemon juice. Place the apples in a 10-inch square baking pan. Repeat with the remaining apples.

Combine the walnuts, brown sugar, cinnamon, and ¼ cup of the syrup in a medium mixing bowl. Stir with a wooden spoon until the liquid is well incorporated and the ingredients look uniformly mixed. Stuff the nut filling into the apples, packing it down tightly, being careful to avoid breaking through the bottom of the fruit.

4 large baking apples, such as Rome or Cortland

1 lemon, halved

1 cup finely chopped walnuts

¼ cup packed light brown sugar

½ teaspoon ground cinnamon

¾ cup Apple Butter Syrup or maple syrup

½ cup orange juice

Combine the remaining ½ cup syrup and the orange juice in a small saucepan and bring the mixture to a boil over high heat, stirring occasionally. Immediately remove the pan from the heat. Spoon the hot liquid over and around the apples in the baking pan.

Bake the apples for 1 hour, basting with the pan juices every 10 to 15 minutes, or until they feel soft when pierced with the tip of a sharp paring knife.

Allow the apples to cool for at least 15 minutes. Serve them warm, topped with 1 to 2 tablespoonfuls of the liquid from the baking pan.

MAKES 4 SERVINGS

Lobster Eggs Benedict

Lobster Eggs Benedict

You can't get much fancier than this for a breakfast or brunch. With a salad of bitter greens, this is a perfect supper dish, too. If you don't want to bother cooking lobsters, you can buy cooked lobster meat at many fish markets and gourmet shops.

TO PREPARE THE LOBSTER MEAT, IF USING LIVE LOBSTERS

Bring a large deep pot of salted water to a boil. Plunge the lobsters head first into the boiling water and cover the pot. Allow the water to return to a boil and cook the lobsters until they are bright red, about 12 minutes. (Remove the lid if the steam rocks the lid wildly.)

Drain the lobsters in a colander placed in the sink. Run cold water over them for 1 minute—or until just cool enough to handle. Twist off the claws and tails and discard the lobster bodies.

Crack the claws with a nutcracker or the back of a heavy cleaver and remove the meat with a long thin fork (a fondue fork works well). Split the underside of each tail open lengthwise with kitchen scissors and remove the tail meat in one piece. Slice the tail meat crosswise about ¼ inch thick. Cover the meat and keep warm.

TO PREPARE THE EGGS

Fill two large skillets half full with water and bring to a simmer over medium heat.

While the water is coming to a simmer, crack each egg into a small bowl, being careful not to break the yolks.

Four ¾-inch slices peasant bread or other hearty bread, toasted

Two 1-pound live lobsters (or ¾ pound cooked lobster)

8 large eggs, at room temperature

For the mustard hollandaise sauce

3 large egg yolks, at room temperature

½ pound unsalted butter (2 sticks), melted and still hot

2 tablespoons Horseradish Mustard or Dijon mustard

2 tablespoons fresh lemon juice

Salt to taste

Cayenne pepper to taste

Gently slip 1 egg into the simmering water. Repeat quickly with the remaining eggs, placing 4 eggs in each skillet. Reduce the heat to low, and poach the eggs until just set, about 3 minutes.

Using a slotted spoon, remove the eggs from the skillets one at a time, and place them on a warm plate lined with paper towels to absorb excess water. Cover the eggs and keep warm.

TO PREPARE THE SAUCE

Place the egg yolks in a blender and quickly pulse on and off to break them up. With the blender running, dribble in 2 tablespoons boiling water through the hole in the lid. With the blender still on, add the hot melted butter in a thin stream and blend until the butter is completely incorporated and the sauce is thick and pale yellow. Add the mustard, lemon juice, salt, and cayenne and blend until smooth.

TO ASSEMBLE THE DISH

Place 1 slice of toast on each of four plates. Top each slice of toast with one-quarter of the warm lobster meat and 2 poached eggs. Spoon about ¼ cup of the hollandaise sauce over the eggs on each plate and serve immediately, with the remaining sauce on the side.

MAKES 4 SERVINGS

Fried Eggs with Curry-Browned Butter and Chutney

Fried Eggs with Curry

Curry powder, which is actually a mix of spices, comes in endless combinations from fiery, hot reds to delicate, sweet golds, but any supermarket variety is just fine here. If you use a mild curry powder, accompany the eggs with a spicy chutney. Alternatively, a mild chutney goes best when using a hotter curry powder, often identified as "Madras-style." Serve the eggs with Spicy Maine Home Fries (page 14) and toasted English muffins.

Melt the butter in a large skillet, preferably nonstick, over medium heat. Continue to cook until the butter turns light brown, about 30 seconds more. Add the curry powder and stir with a wooden spoon to distribute the curry evenly through the butter.

Crack the eggs into the skillet one at a time, leaving a small space between each. Cook until the whites are just set, about 1 minute. Carefully flip each egg—you don't want to break the yolks—and cook until the yolks feel soft but not liquid when pressed gently with your finger, about 1 minute more.

Transfer 2 eggs to each plate, using a spatula. Season with salt, spoon 2 tablespoons of the chutney alongside each serving, and serve immediately.

1 tablespoon unsalted butter

1½ teaspoons curry powder

4 large eggs, at room temperature

Salt to taste

¼ cup Old Farmhouse Chutney or mango chutney

MAKES 2 SERVINGS

Spicy Maine Home Fries

These chunks of spicy potatoes, crisp and golden brown, are a Sunday morning treat for us. Their heat comes from a combination of our Smoky Chipotle Chili Oil and crushed red pepper flakes. If you use regular olive oil, double the amount of pepper flakes, or just increase it to taste. If you prefer your home fries extra crunchy, put the cooked potatoes on a nonstick cookie sheet and bake them for 15 minutes in a preheated 400°F oven.

Place the potatoes in a large saucepan and add enough water to cover by 2 inches. Bring to a boil over high heat and cook the potatoes until they offer just a little resistance when stabbed with the point of a sharp paring knife, about 15 minutes. Drain the potatoes in a colander set in the sink. Allow the potatoes to cool, then cut them into 1-inch chunks.

Heat the oil in a large skillet, preferably cast iron, over medium heat. Add the butter and heat until the butter is melted and foamy. Add the bell pepper and onion and cook, stirring, until the onion is translucent, about 3 minutes.

Stir in the potatoes. Cook without stirring until the potatoes are golden and crusty on the bottom, about 5 minutes. Turn the potatoes, using a spatula or a flat wooden spoon, and continue to cook, turning occasionally, until the potatoes are golden brown all over, about 15 minutes.

Stir in the paprika, celery seeds, pepper flakes, and salt and pepper. Serve immediately.

8 medium red-skinned potatoes (about 1¼ pounds)

2 tablespoons Smoky Chi ve oil

2 tablespoons unsalted butter

1 red bell pepper, cored, seeded, and roughly chopped

1 large onion, roughly chopped

¼ teaspoon sweet paprika

¼ teaspoon celery seeds

¼ to ½ teaspoon crushed red pepper flakes

Salt and freshly ground black pepper to taste

MAKES 4 SERVINGS

Pumpkin-Cranberry Spice Bread

When we made marmalade to sell at our local farmers' market, there would always be some left in the bottom of the pot. In New England, we don't waste anything, so we added the leftover marmalade to sweeten the batter of this versatile quick bread. It's great for breakfast, or with a little honey for a midmorning pick-me-up. Toast it with some butter to complement a cup of late-afternoon hot tea. Or serve it for dessert with vanilla-flavored whipped cream.

Preheat the oven to 350°F. Generously grease a 9 × 5-inch loaf pan.

Beat the sugar with the oil in a large mixing bowl until well combined. Add the eggs and beat until well incorporated. Add the pumpkin and marmalade and beat until smooth.

Combine the flour, salt, baking soda, cinnamon, ginger, nutmeg, and cloves in a medium bowl and whisk until the spices are evenly distributed. Add the flour mixture to the wet ingredients ½ cup at a time, stirring until completely incorporated. Stir in the cranberries and nuts (if using).

Scrape the batter into the prepared loaf pan and bake for 1 hour and 5 minutes, or until a toothpick inserted into the center of the loaf comes out clean. (The loaf will begin to pull away from the sides of the pan when it is done.) Set the pan on a cooling rack for 10 minutes.

Invert the pan to release the bread. Cool it completely on the rack. The bread will keep for up to 2 days at room temperature, wrapped in plastic.

¾ cup sugar

⅓ cup canola oil

2 large eggs

1 cup canned pumpkin puree

½ cup Orange Cranberry Marmalade or orange marmalade

1½ cups plus 2 tablespoons all-purpose flour

½ teaspoon salt

½ teaspoon baking soda

2 teaspoons ground cinnamon

1 teaspoon ground ginger

½ teaspoon grated nutmeg

¼ teaspoon ground cloves

½ cup dried cranberries

¼ cup roughly chopped walnuts, optional

MAKES 1 LOAF

Jelly Omelet

Jelly omelets? For many of us, these are a breakfast tradition. You find them on diner menus up and down the East Coast and across the Midwest. A little patience and a good nonstick pan are the secrets to making omelets at home. Adding a few tablespoonfuls of milk makes a fluffier omelet.

Combine the eggs, milk (if using), and salt in a medium bowl. Beat with a fork or whisk until the eggs are frothy.

Melt the butter in a large skillet, preferably nonstick, over medium heat. Add the eggs and cook without stirring until the edges begin to set, about 30 seconds. Push the cooked edges toward the center with a wooden spoon and tilt the pan so that the uncooked egg runs to the sides, filling the spaces you've just created. Repeat this process once more, shaking the pan occasionally to make sure the omelet is not sticking to the pan. Cook the omelet until the top is set and the bottom is lightly brown, about 2 minutes more. (If you like your eggs very well done, flip the omelet over with a large spatula and cook for another minute.)

Spoon the jelly over half of the omelet, and fold the other half over to cover the jelly.

Carefully slide the omelet onto a serving platter or cutting board. Cut the omelet in half and serve immediately.

5 large eggs, at room temperature

2 tablespoons milk, optional

⅛ teaspoon salt

1 tablespoon plus 1 teaspoon unsalted butter

¼ cup jelly or jam

MAKES 2 SERVINGS

Buttermilk Pancakes

Our pancakes are light and fluffy because we use both baking powder and baking soda, and they're rich due to the buttermilk. We make them with blueberries in season, but you can add thinly sliced peaches, chocolate chips, or any other favorites. Top these off with plenty of butter and one of our syrups, or some warm melted jam.

Combine the flour, sugar, baking powder, and baking soda in a large bowl, stirring until well combined.

Place the buttermilk, eggs, and melted butter in a medium bowl and whisk until well blended. Add to the dry ingredients and stir until just combined. A few small lumps may be visible—that's okay: Do not overmix the batter. Gently fold in the blueberries (if using).

Heat a large skillet over medium heat for 1 minute. Add 1 teaspoon butter to the hot pan and spread it around with a pastry brush or a folded paper towel. For each pancake, pour ¼ cup of batter into the skillet, leaving a few inches between the pancakes, so the batter has room to spread. (If desired, use two skillets simultaneously.) Cook the pancakes until the bottoms are brown and small bubbles that don't close up appear on the surface, about 3 minutes. Flip the pancakes and cook for 1 minute more, or until the bottoms are light brown. Transfer the pancakes to a plate and serve immediately with syrup, or keep warm while you repeat with the remaining batter, adding more butter to the pan between each batch.

Note: To keep the pancakes warm, place them on an ovenproof plate, cover them with foil, and place the plate in a 200°F oven for up to 15 minutes.

2 cups all-purpose flour

2 tablespoons sugar

1 teaspoon baking powder

1 teaspoon baking soda

1¾ cups plus 2 tablespoons buttermilk

2 large eggs, at room temperature

3 tablespoons unsalted butter, melted, plus additional butter for cooking and serving

2 cups blueberries, optional (about 1 pint)

Maine Maple Syrup, Wild Maine Blueberry Syrup, Apple Butter Syrup, or warm jam

MAKES ABOUT 16 PANCAKES

Jam Muffins

If you're like us, you sometimes have any number of jars in your refrigerator with barely enough jam in each to spread on toast. Don't throw them away. Use the jam to make these colorful muffins, baked with a teaspoon of jam inside each one. The jam helps keep the muffins moist, so they'll taste fresh all day.

Preheat the oven to 400°F. Grease a 12-cup muffin tin.

Break the egg into a large mixing bowl and beat it with a fork until foamy. Stir in the milk and butter.

Sift together the flour, cornmeal, sugar, baking powder, and salt. Add to the egg mixture and beat with a wooden spoon just until blended. A few lumps may be visible—that's okay.

Fill the muffin cups one-quarter full with batter. Place 1 teaspoon jam or jelly in the center of each. Cover the jelly with the remaining batter.

Bake for 20 minutes, or until the muffins are light brown. Invert the muffin tins to release the muffins. (You may need to run a small sharp knife around the edge of each muffin first.) Serve warm.

Note: These muffins are best eaten the day they are made. They can be reheated, wrapped in aluminum foil, in a 350°F oven for 10 minutes.

1 large egg, at room temperature

1 cup whole milk

4 tablespoons (½ stick) unsalted butter, melted

1½ cups all-purpose flour

½ cup cornmeal

3 tablespoons sugar

1 tablespoon baking powder

½ teaspoon salt

¼ cup jam or jelly

MAKES 12 MUFFINS

French Toast with Cream Cheese and Jam Filling

Cut a pocket in a thick slice of bread, fill it with cream cheese and jam, dip it in an egg-milk mixture, and fry it like traditional French toast for a real treat. Use a dense egg bread, such as brioche or challah, so you can easily cut pockets in it without its falling apart. For a richer French toast, substitute half-and-half or cream for the milk.

Lay 1 slice of bread on a cutting board. Using a sharp paring knife or small serrated knife, cut a pocket through what was the bottom of the loaf. Be careful not to cut all the way through the bread. Repeat with the remaining slices.

Carefully spread 1 tablespoon of the cream cheese and 1 tablespoon of the jam inside each pocket.

Break the eggs into a large mixing bowl and add the milk, vanilla, and cinnamon (if using). Beat with a fork or a whisk until the eggs are foamy.

Place 1 tablespoon of the butter in a skillet large enough to hold 4 slices of bread in one layer and melt the butter. (Use two skillets simultaneously if desired.) While the butter melts, one at a time, dip 4 slices of stuffed bread into the egg mixture for about 10 seconds, turning or submerging them as necessary so the bread becomes saturated with the egg mixture.

Place the bread into the hot skillet and cook until the bottoms are brown, 1 to 2 minutes. Turn the French toast over and continue to cook until both sides are brown, about 1 minute more. Remove the French toast from the skillet and serve immediately or cover with foil to keep warm. Repeat the process with the remaining bread, adding more butter to the skillet as necessary to keep the French toast from sticking.

Serve the French toast warm, dusted with the confectioners' sugar.

Eight 1½-inch slices egg bread

4 ounces cream cheese, at room temperature

½ cup boysenberry jam, grape jelly, or other jam or jelly

8 large eggs

½ cup whole milk

1 teaspoon vanilla extract

½ teaspoon ground cinnamon, optional

2 tablespoons unsalted butter, plus more if needed

¼ cup confectioners' sugar

MAKES 4 SERVINGS

Jelly Doughnuts

Stop in at any country store in New England and you're sure to find homemade doughnuts on the counter. Since they're only good when freshly made, we decided to make our own doughnuts, filled, of course, with our own jelly. They do take time to make, as the dough needs to rise twice, but they are well worth it. We deep-fry them quickly, so they don't absorb a lot of oil, making the lightest jelly doughnuts we've ever tasted.

Combine the yeast and 1 tablespoon of the granulated sugar in a large mixing bowl. Heat the milk in a small pan over low heat until it is just warm to the touch. Add the milk to the yeast and stir until the yeast and sugar dissolve. Allow the yeast to proof for 5 minutes, or until it is foamy.

Add the eggs, melted butter, ⅓ cup of the granulated sugar, and salt to the yeast mixture and stir until well blended. Stir in 4 cups flour, ½ cup at a time, until a soft dough forms. Turn the dough out onto the counter and knead until it is smooth and elastic, about 10 minutes. Add more flour as necessary to keep the dough from sticking to your hands and the counter.

Place the dough in a well-buttered bowl and turn the dough to coat the entire surface with butter. Cover the bowl with plastic wrap or a clean kitchen towel and let rise in a warm, draft-free area until the dough has doubled in bulk, about 45 minutes.

Punch down the dough using your fist, and turn it out onto the counter. Divide it into 2 pieces, one about 1¼ times as large as the other. One at a time, roll both pieces out to a thickness of ¼ inch. Using cookie cutters or inverted glasses, cut twelve 3-inch circles from the smaller piece of dough and twelve 4-inch circles from the larger piece.

Place 1 level tablespoon of jelly in the middle of one 3-inch circle of dough. Dip your finger in a small bowl of cold water and wet the perimeter of the

Ingredients

3 tablespoons active dry yeast

⅓ cup plus 1 tablespoon granulated sugar

1 cup whole milk

2 large eggs, lightly beaten

8 tablespoons (1 stick) unsalted butter, melted, plus additional butter, at room temperature, for the bowl

½ teaspoon salt

4 to 5 cups all-purpose flour

1 cup jelly or jam

4 cups canola oil, for deep-frying

¼ cup confectioners' sugar

circle. Place a 4-inch circle over the jelly and press the edges of the dough together. Pick up the filled doughnut and crimp the edge all around—a tight seal ensures that the jelly doesn't leak out when the doughnut is fried. Place the doughnut on a floured cutting board or nonstick cookie sheet and repeat with the remaining circles of dough and jelly. Cover the doughnuts with a clean kitchen towel and let them rise for 30 minutes, or until nearly doubled in bulk.

Pour the oil into a wok or large heavy pot deep enough to hold 4 inches of oil. Clip a candy or deep-frying thermometer to the inside of the pan and place the pan over medium-high heat.

When the oil reaches 350°F, uncover the doughnuts and reseal any edges that may have opened. Carefully slide 3 or 4 doughnuts at a time into the hot oil. Do not add too many to the pan, or they will not cook properly. Turn the doughnuts when they are light brown on the bottom, after about 1 minute. Cook for 1 minute more or until the doughnuts are golden all over. Remove the doughnuts from the oil with a slotted spoon and place them on a plate lined with paper towels to drain.

Let the doughnuts cool for at least 5 minutes. Sift the confectioners' sugar over the tops and serve. The doughnuts are best the day they are made. **MAKES 12 DOUGHNUTS**

Soups and Sandwiches

When we were young, our mothers served us soup-and-a-sandwich to warm us in the winter after a snowball fight. These were not elaborate meals. After all, our mothers' pantries were stocked with hot dog mustard, mayonnaise, and canned tomato soup.

Our soup and sandwich recipes reflect today's pantry. Our soups have been souped up with Marinated Sun-Dried Tomatoes, crunchy relishes, and herbed jams. Mustards and chutneys with international flavors have replaced our mothers' simple sandwich condiments. A well-stocked pantry can help bring new life to almost any good old soup or sandwich recipe.

Roast Beef with Old Farmhouse Chutney on Rye is a fresh take on an old favorite. And a Gooey Grilled Cheddar-Bacon Sandwich becomes a new classic with the addition of Onion & Jalapeño Mustard. Try a refreshing summer soup with fresh mangoes and peaches and Ginger Peach Tea Jam. Add Corn Relish to further elevate Corn-Crab Chowder to dinner-party status.

Corn-Crab Chowder

There are as many versions of chowder (pronounced *chow*-da) in Maine as there are Downeasters (what the locals are called) and everyone claims their recipe is the best. We're partial to this one that calls for crab and corn. What makes it extra special is the dollop of spicy Corn Relish, which adds both texture and heat in one heaping spoonful.

Melt the butter in a large pot over medium heat. Sauté the onions and celery until the onions are translucent and the celery is softened, about 5 minutes. Add the potatoes, corn, garlic, and thyme and cook for 1 minute, stirring constantly.

Add the vermouth and raise the heat to high. Allow the vermouth to come to a boil, and cook until the pan is almost dry. Pour the chicken stock into the pot, bring to a boil, and add the bay leaf. Reduce the heat to medium and simmer the soup, uncovered, for 20 minutes, or until the potatoes are just tender when pierced with the tip of a sharp knife. Remove from the heat and allow the soup to cool for 10 minutes.

Remove and discard the bay leaf, then puree the soup in two or three batches in a blender or food processor. (There is no need to scrape down the sides of the blender—a few small chunks of vegetables will give a nice texture to the soup.) The soup can be made to this point and kept covered in the refrigerator for up to 2 days.

Return the soup to the pot and bring to a simmer over medium-low heat. Add the crab, cream, and cilantro. Cook just long enough to heat the crab through, about 3 minutes. Season with salt and pepper.

Ladle the soup into bowls and top each serving with 1 heaping tablespoon of the corn relish. Serve immediately.

3 tablespoons unsalted butter

2 small white onions, finely chopped

1 large celery stalk, finely chopped

½ pound small waxy potatoes, peeled and quartered

3 cups fresh (cut from about 5 medium ears corn) or frozen corn kernels

1 large garlic clove, minced

1 teaspoon fresh thyme leaves or ¼ teaspoon dried thyme

¼ cup white vermouth or dry white wine

4 cups chicken stock or canned low-sodium broth

1 bay leaf

2 cups (16 ounces) lump crabmeat, picked over for shells and cartilage

½ cup heavy cream

¼ cup finely chopped cilantro

Salt and freshly ground black pepper to taste

1 cup Corn Relish or your favorite vegetable relish

MAKES 6 TO 8 SERVINGS

Peach-Mango Soup

This cold, smooth, not-too-sweet fruit soup is a perfect first course in summer, served with a flute of Champagne, but it also makes a light finish to any meal, accompanied by a plate of amaretti or Pecan Sandies. Another suggestion: Omit the crème fraîche and serve the soup warm, with a small scoop of vanilla ice cream in the center of each bowl.

Place the peaches and mangoes in a medium saucepan. Add the wine and 1 cup water and bring to a simmer over medium heat. Cook until the fruit is tender and starting to fall apart, about 7 minutes. Allow the soup to cool for 10 minutes.

Puree the soup with the jam in a food processor or blender, stopping occasionally to scrape down the sides to ensure a smooth puree. Pour into a medium bowl or a pitcher, cover, and refrigerate until cold. The soup can be prepared to this point up to 2 days in advance.

Stir the lemon juice and salt into the soup. Pour or ladle the soup into four bowls, top each serving with 1 tablespoon of the crème fraîche, and garnish with a mint sprig. Serve immediately.

4 small peaches (about 1 pound), peeled, quartered, and pitted

2 small mangoes (about 1½ pounds), peeled, pitted, and roughly chopped

1 cup dry white wine or white vermouth

½ cup Ginger Peach Tea Jam or ½ cup peach jam plus ½ teaspoon ground ginger

Juice of 1 lemon, strained

¼ teaspoon salt

¼ cup crème fraîche or yogurt

4 mint sprigs

MAKES 4 SERVINGS

Year-Round Gazpacho

Year-Round Gazpacho

Gazpacho, a cold and crunchy summer tomato soup, is traditionally made with peak-of-the-season, vine-ripened tomatoes, but using our Marinated Sun-Dried Tomatoes makes it possible to serve this favorite year-round. A generous drizzle of Sun-Dried Tomato Basil Oil just before serving heightens the intense tomato flavor. Make the soup a day ahead if possible to allow the flavors to blend. Serve it with a basket of crusty bread.

Combine the tomato juice, vegetable broth, vinegar, lemon juice, Worcestershire, Tabasco, sun-dried tomatoes, celery, onion, red pepper, and cucumber in a large bowl and stir until well combined. Cover and refrigerate for at least 8 hours or overnight.

Season the soup with salt and pepper. Ladle it into serving bowls and drizzle each serving with 1½ teaspoons of the oil. Serve immediately.

3 cups tomato juice or V-8 juice

1 cup canned vegetable broth

2 tablespoons cider vinegar

2 tablespoons fresh lemon juice, strained

1 teaspoon Worcestershire sauce

⅛ teaspoon Tabasco sauce

1 cup minced Marinated Sun-Dried Tomatoes

1 cup minced celery

¼ cup minced red onion

1 red bell pepper, cored, seeded, and minced

1 small cucumber, peeled, seeded, and minced

Salt and freshly ground black pepper to taste

3 to 4 tablespoons Sun-Dried Tomato Basil Oil or olive oil

MAKES 6 TO 8 SERVINGS

Gooey Grilled Cheddar-Bacon Sandwiches

Sharp Cheddar and smoky bacon make a comforting grilled cheese sandwich. But when we add just a touch of our Onion & Jalapeño Mustard, we create a grilled cheese sandwich that redefines comfort food.

Divide the cheese equally between 2 slices of the bread, breaking or cutting it to fit the bread if necessary. Top the cheese with the bacon.

Spread 1 tablespoon of the mustard on each of the remaining 2 slices of bread. Place them mustard side down on top of the bacon and cheese.

Melt the butter in a large skillet over medium heat. Place the sandwiches in the pan and cook until the bottom of the sandwiches turns a light golden brown and the cheese begins to melt, about 2 minutes. Carefully flip the sandwiches over and cook, adding additional butter to the pan if necessary, until the second side turns a light golden brown and the cheese is completely melted, about 2 minutes more.

Cut each sandwich in half and serve.

6 ounces Cheddar, thinly sliced

4 slices rye bread

4 slices thick-cut bacon, cooked until crisp and drained

2 tablespoons Onion & Jalapeño Mustard or strong flavored mustard

1½ tablespoons unsalted butter, plus more if needed

MAKES 2 SANDWICHES

Stonewall Lobster Rolls

Stonewall Lobster Rolls

As soon as you cross the Piscataqua River from New Hampshire into Maine, you will see signs all along U.S. Route 1 touting lobster rolls, served at the trailers, shacks, and diners that line the coastal road. A traditional lobster roll is nothing more than cooked, fresh lobster meat combined with mayonnaise, served on a toasted hot dog bun with a side of potato chips. We like to add a touch of our Lemon Dill Cocktail Sauce as well. Some folks insist that the hot dog bun should be fried rather than toasted. If you're among them, butter the split buns, place them buttered side down on a hot griddle or pan, and cook until they are light brown and crisp.

Chop the lobster meat into small pieces; do not chop it too fine—the perfect lobster roll has small chunks of meat in it.

Place the lobster in a medium mixing bowl. Add the mayonnaise and cocktail sauce and gently toss just until the lobster is well coated. Season with salt and pepper. The lobster can be prepared to this point up to 24 hours in advance. Keep covered and refrigerated.

Pile the lobster into the toasted hot dog buns and serve immediately.

¾ pound cooked lobster meat (from two 1-pound lobsters)

3 tablespoons mayonnaise

1½ tablespoons Lemon Dill Cocktail Sauce or your favorite cocktail sauce

Salt and freshly ground black pepper to taste

2 hot dog buns, toasted in a toaster oven or under the broiler

MAKES 2 SANDWICHES

Roasted Eggplant and Smoked Mozzarella Sandwiches

The beaches in the Yorks, Ogunquit, and Kennebunkport, along Maine's southern coast, overflow with tourists in the summer, but in late spring or early autumn they are quiet, tranquil places to walk or picnic. We pack these Italian vegetarian sandwiches, along with a bottle of red wine or sparkling cider, to take to the beach with friends when they come for an off-season visit.

Preheat the oven to 400°F.

Lightly brush both sides of the eggplant slices with the olive oil. Place the slices on a baking sheet large enough to hold them in one layer, and season with salt and pepper.

Roast the eggplant for 30 minutes, or until the slices are softened and just starting to brown. Remove from the oven and allow the eggplant to cool completely.

Meanwhile, turn the oven up to broil. Slice the rolls in half and place them cut side up under the broiler for 20 to 30 seconds, until lightly browned; keep a careful eye on them because they burn quickly. Remove them from the broiler and rub the cut sides with the garlic clove.

Divide the eggplant slices among the bottom halves of the rolls. Top each with an equal amount of the cheese and 2 tablespoons of the relish. Place the tops on the sandwiches and press lightly with your hands to flatten the sandwiches slightly. The sandwiches can be enjoyed immediately or made 4 to 6 hours in advance and kept at room temperature, wrapped in plastic.

1 large eggplant (about 1½ pounds), cut into ¼-inch slices

¼ cup extra virgin olive oil

Salt and freshly ground black pepper to taste

4 medium crusty rolls

1 garlic clove, peeled

½ pound smoked mozzarella, thinly sliced

½ cup Sun-Dried Tomato and Olive Relish or Marinated Sun-Dried Tomatoes, drained

MAKES 4 SANDWICHES

Southwest Shrimp Wraps

Maine lobsters grow large, but our shrimp are usually small. So we use the larger shrimp flown in from the Gulf Coast, the Florida coast, or Asia. You can find these shrimp cooked and ready-to-eat in most supermarkets and fish stores. Two tips for making these wraps: The first is our Corn Relish, which gives them a bit of Southwestern flavor and spice. The second is to fold the tortillas tightly to seal in the freshness, so you can make them ahead.

Place 1 lettuce leaf in the middle of each tortilla and top with 4 shrimp, one-quarter of the avocado slices, 2 tablespoons of the corn relish, a few onion rings, and 1 tablespoon of the cilantro.

Fold the sides of each tortilla over, leaving some of the filling exposed. Fold the bottom up over the filling and roll up the tortilla, creating a bundle that resembles a burrito or large egg roll.

Wrap the sandwiches tightly in plastic and refrigerate until ready to serve. The wraps can be enjoyed immediately or made up to 4 hours in advance.

4 large red-tipped lettuce leaves or romaine lettuce leaves

4 large flour tortillas

16 large peeled, cooked, and deveined shrimp (about 1 pound)

1 large ripe avocado, peeled, pitted, and thinly sliced

½ cup Corn Relish

1 small red onion, thinly sliced and separated into rings

¼ cup coarsely chopped cilantro

MAKES 4 SANDWICHES

Egg Salad on Black Bread

This is no ordinary egg salad sandwich. We got the idea from Jim's dad, who always added a little horseradish to his egg salad and served it on New England black bread. If horseradish made egg salad tasty, we thought some Horseradish Mustard would make it even better. It did. If you don't have any on hand, use Dijon mustard and add a tablespoon of prepared horseradish.

Place the eggs in a medium saucepan and add cold water to cover them by 2 inches. Bring the water to a full rolling boil over high heat and boil the eggs for exactly 4 minutes. (Be careful not to overcook the eggs, or they may develop a green ring around the yolk.) Remove the pan from the heat and set aside for 4 minutes. Drain the eggs and run cold water over them until they are cool.

Combine the mayonnaise, mustard, scallions, celery, and pickle in a medium bowl, stirring until well blended.

Peel and coarsely chop the eggs. Add them to the mayonnaise mixture and toss gently, just until the eggs are evenly coated. Season with salt and pepper.

Spoon about ¾ cup of the egg salad onto 1 slice of black bread and spread it evenly to the edges. Cover the egg salad with ¼ cup of the radicchio (if using). Top with another slice of bread and cut the sandwich diagonally in half. Repeat with the remaining egg salad, bread, and radicchio. Serve immediately.

8 large eggs

½ cup mayonnaise

¼ cup Horseradish Mustard

2 scallions, thinly sliced

1 celery stalk, minced

1 dill pickle, minced

Salt and freshly ground black pepper to taste

8 thick slices black bread or pumpernickel

1 cup shredded radicchio, optional

MAKES 4 SANDWICHES

Smoked Turkey with Roasted Garlic & Onion Jam on Baguette

Roasted Garlic & Onion Jam was one of the first preserves we sold at the farmer's market, and it remains one of our favorites. It seems it's everyone else's too, since this is one of our best-selling products. Drive by Stonewall Kitchen on U.S. Route 1 on a day we're cooking and bottling it, and you can smell the aroma.

Cut each baguette in half, then slice each piece horizontally in half. Divide the turkey evenly among the bottom halves of the baguette slices. Spoon 2 tablespoons of jam on top of each portion of turkey and top with a lettuce leaf. Place the tops on the sandwiches.

Slice the sandwiches in half and serve, or wrap them in wax paper or plastic wrap and let sit at room temperature for no more than 2 hours before serving.

Two 16-inch baguettes

1½ pounds smoked turkey, thickly sliced (about ¼-inch slices)

½ cup Roasted Garlic & Onion Jam or mango chutney

4 small romaine lettuce leaves

MAKES 4 SANDWICHES

Roast Beef with Old Farmhouse Chutney on Rye

If we've had roast beef for dinner, we'll surely have these sandwiches for lunch the next day. Our Old Farmhouse Chutney adds a little spice, but any fruit chutney is good with roast beef. Add some sharp Gorgonzola or aged Cheddar for an even heartier sandwich.

Divide the roast beef evenly among 4 slices of the rye bread. Top each portion with 2 or 3 tomato slices, 3 arugula leaves, and 2 tablespoons of the chutney. Top with the remaining bread and serve, or wrap in wax paper and keep refrigerated for up to 4 hours before serving.

- 1½ pounds cold rare roast beef, thinly sliced
- 8 slices country rye (with or without seeds)
- 2 large beefsteak tomatoes, thinly sliced
- 12 arugula leaves
- ½ cup Old Farmhouse Chutney or fruit chutney

MAKES 4 SANDWICHES

Appetizers

When it comes to appetizers, hearty mustards, spicy chutneys, savory relishes, and zesty sauces can all be timesaving ways to add flavor to your cooking. For quick and easy appetizers, many of our products can be served right from the jar with crackers, breadsticks, or raw vegetables. Here we offer some inventive appetizers to serve with drinks before dinner, or to put together for an entire meal.

Shrimp and Chicken Satay with Two Dipping Sauces

Satays, meat or seafood grilled on bamboo skewers, are a favorite Southeast Asian street food. We suggest shrimp and chicken, but pork loin, beef tenderloin, or even lobster tail meat will work just fine. Satays are always served with a dipping sauce—traditionally a spicy peanut sauce like our Roasted Garlic Peanut Sauce. We like to serve two sauces, both the peanut sauce and our Maple Chipotle Grille Sauce. If you don't have either on hand, use any of our flavored mustards instead.

Preheat the broiler and, if possible, adjust the rack so it sits 3 inches from the heat source.

Remove any cartilage or fat from the chicken and cut each breast lengthwise into 4 strips. Combine the chicken and shrimp in a medium bowl, add the oil, and toss to coat. Add the spice rub and mix with your hands until the chicken and shrimp are well coated.

Thread 1 piece of chicken onto each of 8 of the skewers. Thread 1 shrimp onto each of the remaining 8 skewers. Broil the chicken and shrimp for 4 minutes on each side, or until golden brown. (If the skewers start to burn, cover the exposed bamboo with aluminum foil.)

Serve the satay hot or at room temperature, with small bowls of the dipping sauces on the side.

2 boneless, skinless chicken breasts (about ¾ pound)

8 jumbo shrimp, peeled and deveined (about ½ pound)

2 tablespoons extra virgin olive oil

1 tablespoon Spice Rub for Vegetables or your favorite seasoning mixture

¾ cup Roasted Garlic Peanut Sauce, for dipping

¾ cup Maple Chipotle Grille Sauce, for dipping

Sixteen 10-inch bamboo skewers, soaked for 15 minutes and drained

MAKES 6 TO 8 SERVINGS

Mango-Brie Quesadillas

Quesadillas are Mexican appetizers or snacks, often made with flour tortillas that are filled with a mild white cheese and often a vegetable or two, or beans, or a combination. The tortillas are folded over into turnovers and grilled, broiled, or fried just until slightly crisp and the cheese melts. Our version, made with Brie, roasted peppers, and Mango Salsa sandwiched between two tortillas, is a little more sophisticated, and can be served with cocktails before dinner or with a crisp green salad for a satisfying lunch.

3 red bell peppers

1 pound Brie

Twelve 8-inch flour tortillas

¾ cup Mango Salsa or other fruit salsa

¼ cup roughly chopped cilantro

Roast the peppers directly over a high flame on top of the stove, turning them with long-handled tongs as necessary, until they are charred all over. Alternatively, you can place the peppers under the broiler, about 3 inches from the heat source, and cook, turning the peppers as necessary until the skin is blackened all over. Place the peppers in a paper bag, seal the bag, and let the peppers sit for 30 minutes, or until cooled and softened.

Pull off the skin from the peppers; it will slip off easily. Remove as much charred skin as you can, but it's okay if a few specks remain. Rinse your hands as necessary, but don't rinse the peppers, or you will lose some of the flavor. Cut off the tops of the peppers and discard. Remove the seeds and white membranes with your fingers, and slice each pepper into 8 strips.

Preheat the broiler.

Remove the rind from the Brie and tear the cheese into 24 small pieces. The pieces will not be even, but that's okay. Place 6 of the tortillas on a baking sheet. Place 4 pieces of cheese on each. Top each with 4 strips of roasted red pepper and 2 tablespoons of the salsa. Cover with the remaining tortillas and press down lightly with the palm of your hand to flatten slightly.

Broil the quesadillas 4 inches from the heat until they just start to turn brown in spots, about 2 minutes. Carefully flip each one over, using a spatula, and broil for another 2 minutes, or until the tops have just begun to brown and the cheese is melted.

Transfer the quesadillas to a cutting board, using the spatula, and cut each one into quarters. Sprinkle with the cilantro and serve immediately.

MAKES 6 SERVINGS

Cocktail Shrimp with Roasted Garlic Mayonnaise

What could be more elegant than a martini glass filled with a tangy dipping sauce, half a dozen coral-colored shrimp balanced on its rim? Okay, maybe a large platter of shrimp fanned out in a decorative design with a goblet of dipping sauce on the side. Leave the tips of the tail shells on the shrimp when you peel them, making it easy for your guests to pick them up.

Peel the shrimp, leaving the tips of the tails intact. Place the shrimp in a large bowl of ice water and set aside.

Combine the onion, celery, spice rub, and peppercorns in a medium saucepan. Add the wine and 2 cups water, bring to a boil over high heat, and cook for 10 minutes.

Remove the vegetables with a slotted spoon and discard them. Add the shrimp and cook until they are pink and firm, about 3 minutes. Remove the shrimp with a slotted spoon and plunge them into the ice water to cool. Remove the shrimp and drain on paper towels. The shrimp can be prepared up to 24 hours ahead and kept covered in the refrigerator.

Serve the shrimp cold, alongside a bowl of the mayonnaise or cocktail sauce.

24 jumbo shrimp (about 1½ pounds)

1 onion, quartered

1 celery stalk, roughly chopped

1 tablespoon Spice Rub for Seafood or your favorite spice mixture

10 whole peppercorns

2 cups dry white wine

1¼ cups Roasted Garlic Mayonnaise (recipe follows) or Lemon Dill Cocktail Sauce

MAKES 6 TO 8 SERVINGS

Roasted Garlic Mayonnaise

This can be made up to 2 days ahead of time and kept tightly covered in the refrigerator.

Combine the vinaigrette, mayonnaise, shallots, parsley, and tarragon in a small bowl and stir until well combined. Cover and refrigerate until ready to use.

½ cup Roasted Garlic Vinaigrette

½ cup mayonnaise

¼ cup minced shallots

3 tablespoons minced flat-leaf parsley

2 teaspoons minced tarragon

MAKES ABOUT 1¼ CUPS

Savory Herbed Nuts

These pecans are sautéed in butter to bring out their flavor, and then they're sprinkled with herbs. Pecan halves are perfect for this recipe because they have deep ridges that help trap the herbs. Serve these with cocktails before dinner or with a cheese course instead of dessert. Although the nuts will keep for a few days, they're best when freshly made.

Melt the butter in a large skillet over medium heat. Add the pecans and cook, stirring frequently, until they are lightly toasted and fragrant, about 3 minutes. (Lower the heat if the butter begins to burn.) Add the spice rub and stir to coat the nuts completely. Continue to cook for 1 minute, stirring and shaking the pan constantly.

Remove from the heat and allow the nuts to cool for at least 10 minutes before serving.

Serve the nuts warm, or spread them on a baking sheet and allow to cool completely before storing. The nuts will keep for up to 1 week in an airtight container at room temperature.

4 tablespoons (½ stick) unsalted butter

4 cups (1 pound) pecan halves

¼ cup Spice Rub for Vegetables or your favorite spice mixture

MAKES 4 CUPS

Spicy White Bean Dip

White beans can be bland, but pureed with some hearty mustard and spices they make a flavor-packed dip. You can cook dried beans for this recipe if you feel so inspired, but canned beans, well rinsed, work just fine. Serve this dip with warmed pita bread that has been cut into quarters, or hollow out a round crusty bread and fill it with the dip. Spread some dip on toasted baguette rounds and top each with a cooked shrimp or a Marinated Sun-Dried Tomato.

Combine the beans, mustard, chili powder, cumin, and garlic in a food processor, and pulse until the beans are pureed. With the machine running, slowly pour the oil through the feed tube, processing until the mixture is smooth. Season with salt. The dip can be served immediately, or covered and refrigerated for up to 4 days; bring to room temperature before serving.

Transfer the dip to a serving bowl and sprinkle with the chopped parsley just before serving.

Two 15-ounce cans cannellini beans, drained and rinsed

¼ cup plus 2 table-spoons Onion & Jalapeño Mustard or other flavored mustard

2 teaspoons chili powder

1 teaspoon ground cumin

1 garlic clove, quartered

¼ cup extra virgin olive oil

Salt to taste

2 tablespoons finely chopped flat-leaf parsley

MAKES ABOUT 2½ CUPS

Sun-Dried Tomato Salsa

Chunky, sweet, and tangy, this salsa is perfect with tortilla chips. It's also versatile enough to serve alongside some grilled meat or fish, or spooned on top of scrambled eggs for breakfast or brunch. Make the salsa at least an hour ahead so the flavors can blend.

Combine the beans, sun-dried tomatoes, orange segments, scallions, cilantro, oil, lime juice, and nutmeg in a medium bowl. Toss until well combined. Season with salt and pepper. Cover and refrigerate for at least 1 hour before serving.

Note: This salsa is best eaten within 24 hours.

One 15-ounce can black beans, drained and rinsed

1 cup coarsely chopped drained Marinated Sun-Dried Tomatoes (marinating oil reserved)

¼ cup canned mandarin orange segments, drained and coarsely chopped

6 whole scallions, thinly sliced

¾ cup coarsely chopped cilantro

3 tablespoons reserved Marinated Sun-Dried Tomato oil (from above)

Juice of 1 lime

¼ teaspoon grated nutmeg

Salt and freshly ground black pepper to taste

MAKES ABOUT 3½ CUPS

Sweet and Savory Crostini

Crostini means little toasts in Italian. All these small rounds of bread need are toppings for last-minute appetizers. At home, we blend our mustards and jams with butter or cream cheese, but you can use almost any condiment straight out of the jar if you prefer. Here are just a few suggestions.

Preheat the broiler.

Place the slices of bread on a cookie sheet in one layer. (Toast the bread in batches if necessary.) Place the cookie sheet under the broiler until the bread just begins to turn light brown. This will take only 20 to 30 seconds, so be careful not to burn the bread. Allow the toasts to cool completely before adding the toppings.

SMOKED OYSTER TOPPING

Blend the butter and mustard until thoroughly combined. Spread 1 teaspoon of the mixture on each of 12 toasted rounds. Top each with 1 smoked oyster. Serve immediately.

CURRIED PROSCIUTTO TOPPING

Blend the butter and mustard in a small bowl until thoroughly combined. Spread 1 teaspoon of the mixture on each of 12 toasted rounds. Top each with a small piece of prosciutto. Serve immediately.

SMOKED SALMON TOPPING

Blend the cream cheese and jam in a small bowl until thoroughly combined. Spread 1 teaspoon of the mixture on each of 12 toasted rounds. Top each with 1 small piece of salmon. Serve immediately.

WALNUT CHERRY TOPPING

Blend the cream cheese and jam in a small bowl until thoroughly combined. Spread 1 teaspoon of the mixture on each of 12 toasted rounds. Top each with 1 walnut. Serve immediately.

1 French baguette or Italian bread, at least 16 inches long, cut into ⅓-inch slices

Smoked Oyster Topping

2 tablespoons unsalted butter, at room temperature

2 tablespoons Sesame Ginger Mustard

12 smoked oysters

Curried Prosciutto Topping

2 tablespoons unsalted butter, at room temperature

2 tablespoons Curried Apricot Mustard

2 ounces thinly sliced prosciutto, cut into 12 pieces

Smoked Salmon Topping

3 tablespoons cream cheese, at room temperature

1 tablespoon Tomato Ginger Jam

2 ounces thinly sliced smoked salmon, cut into 12 pieces

Walnut Cherry Topping

3 tablespoons cream cheese

1 tablespoon Cherry Chipotle Jam

12 walnut halves, lightly toasted

MAKES ABOUT 48 CROSTINI

Appetizers **57**

Spiced Scones with Smoked Ham and Cherry Chipotle Jam

Scones are not just for breakfast or teatime anymore. Here, herbed scones, flaky and moist, are split and filled with ham and some chunky sweet/hot jam. Serve the scones with fruit punch or cocktails that are on the sweet side, such as Raspberry Cosmopolitans (page 154) or Stonewall Margaritas (page 152).

Position a rack in the lower third of the oven and preheat the oven to 425°F. Line a large rimmed baking sheet with parchment paper.

Combine the flour, sugar, baking powder, salt, baking soda, ginger, and cloves in a large mixing bowl and whisk until well blended. Add the cold butter to the flour mixture, and cut it in using a pastry blender or two knives—the dough should resemble small peas. Add the buttermilk and stir just until it is absorbed.

Turn the mixture out onto a lightly floured surface and knead until a soft dough forms; do not overwork it. Divide the dough into 4 pieces. One at a time, roll each piece out to a thickness of ½ inch (about 8 inches in diameter). Cut the dough into 1-inch circles using a small cookie cutter or an inverted cordial glass. Reroll the scraps. Place the scones 2 inches apart on the baking sheet.

Combine the marmalade with the 1 tablespoon room-temperature butter in a small bowl and stir until well blended. Brush 1½ tablespoons of the marmalade mixture over each scone. Bake for 10 minutes, or until the scones are golden on both top and bottom and sound hollow when tapped.

Cool the scones on a wire rack. They can be made up to 8 hours in advance and kept wrapped in a kitchen towel. To serve, split each scone horizontally and cover the bottom half with a small piece of smoked ham. Spoon 1 teaspoon of the jam over the ham and cover with the top of the scone.

For the scones

3 cups all-purpose flour

⅓ cup sugar

2½ teaspoons baking powder

¾ teaspoon salt

½ teaspoon baking soda

½ teaspoon ground ginger

¼ teaspoon ground cloves

12 tablespoons (1½ sticks) cold unsalted butter, cut into ½-inch cubes, plus 1 tablespoon unsalted butter, at room temperature

1 cup buttermilk

¼ cup Orange-Cranberry Marmalade or orange marmalade

2 pounds smoked ham, sliced ¼ inch thick and cut into 1-inch squares

1 cup Cherry Chipotle Jam or Red Pepper Jelly

MAKES ABOUT 48 SCONES

Pastas
and Salads

Our kitchen in York, Maine, is located on U.S. Route 1 just off I-95 and you can stop by seven days a week. We've created a welcoming complex with an herb garden and an open test kitchen. It also houses our home office and our flagship store, where we spend time every day greeting our customers. Between new product tastings, talking with local growers, and trying to meet as many customers as possible, we don't always want to spend hours cooking dinner after work. Who does? But we still want a satisfying meal at the end of the day.

The answers lie in using our own jars of relishes, mustards, oils, and chutneys. These condiments can dress up simple salads and turn familiar pasta standbys into satisfying comfort food.

Baked Macaroni and Cheese has more depth and character with some Sun-Dried Tomato Mustard. And Thai Peanut Noodle Salad is one of the easiest pasta dishes to prepare when you add our Roasted Garlic Peanut Sauce right from the jar. Try our fast but savory Penne with Fennel, Lemon, and Pine Nuts. Or our Smoked Trout Salad with Cranberry Horseradish Vinaigrette. All of our salads and pastas use condiments to complement the taste of the fresh ingredients, not overwhelm them. This is pantry cooking at its finest.

Angel Hair with Walnut Pesto

Although pesto is traditionally made with pine nuts, we like to use the more readily available walnuts. Serve pesto on pasta, as a dip, or spread it on toasted rounds of thinly sliced bread. Before storing the pesto, pour a little olive oil on the surface to seal out air or place a piece of plastic wrap directly on the surface to keep it from discoloring. The pesto keeps well for a week, tightly covered in the refrigerator.

Combine the basil, garlic, olive oil, and salt in a food processor and pulse on and off until the mixture begins to come together, then process until the basil is pureed. Stop the machine, scrape down the sides, and add the walnuts and cheese. Process until the pesto is smooth, about 30 seconds. The pesto can be made ahead and kept tightly covered in the refrigerator for up to a week.

Place the pesto in a large bowl and set it aside.

Bring 6 quarts salted water to a boil in a large stockpot over high heat. Add the pasta, return the water to a boil, and cook the pasta for 3 to 4 minutes, or until it is just tender. Reserve ¼ cup of the pasta cooking water and drain the pasta.

Add the pasta, along with the reserved cooking water, to the pesto. Toss until the pasta is well coated. Serve immediately.

4 cups packed basil leaves

2 large garlic cloves, quartered

⅔ cup extra virgin olive oil

½ teaspoon salt, or to taste

½ cup walnut pieces

½ cup freshly grated Parmigiano-Reggiano

1½ pounds angel hair pasta

MAKES 6 SERVINGS

Spicy Linguine with Shrimp

As immigrants settled in Maine to work in the thriving shipping and fishing industries, international flavors found their way into traditional New England cooking. This spicy tomato pasta dish is an Italian favorite made with Maine shrimp, which are very small (35 or more shrimp per pound), and jazzed up with our Roasted Garlic Oil. Rock shrimp are the perfect alternative, but any shrimp will work.

Preheat the oven to 500°F.

Slice the tomatoes in half and place them cut side down in an oiled roasting pan large enough to hold them in one layer. Scatter the garlic cloves over the tomatoes, and sprinkle with the salt.

Bake for 30 minutes, or until the tomato skins begin to turn brown. For a stronger flavor, place the tomatoes under the broiler for 1 minute.

Transfer the tomatoes and garlic with all the accumulated juices to a food processor. Add the red pepper flakes, garlic oil, and parsley and pulse on and off until the sauce is smooth. The sauce can be made up to 3 days ahead of time and kept tightly covered in the refrigerator.

Pour the sauce into a large saucepan or skillet set over medium heat and bring to a simmer. Add the shrimp and stir constantly until the shrimp curl and turn pink, about 3 minutes. Turn off the heat.

Meanwhile, bring 4 quarts salted water to a boil in a large stockpot over high heat. Add the pasta, return the water to a boil, and cook the pasta for 4 minutes, or until it is just tender. Drain and add it to the sauce.

Turn the heat under the pan up to high and toss the pasta with the sauce until the shrimp are heated through, about 1 minute. Serve immediately.

12 large plum tomatoes

6 garlic cloves, halved

1 teaspoon kosher salt

½ teaspoon crushed red pepper flakes, or to taste

¼ cup Roasted Garlic Oil or olive oil

8 flat-leaf parsley sprigs

1 pound rock shrimp or small shrimp (more than 30–35 per pound), peeled and deveined

1 pound linguine

MAKES 4 SERVINGS

Baked Macaroni and Cheese

Rich and gooey, hearty and filling, mac and cheese is the ultimate comfort food. Use any cheese or any combination of cheese you like, provided there's a total of ¾ pound. Some purists insist on only sharp Cheddar, but we combine cheeses. We also add some Stonewall Kitchen Sun-Dried Tomato Mustard, giving this old classic a new twist.

Preheat the oven to 350°F. Generously butter a 2-quart casserole or soufflé dish.

Melt the butter in a large saucepan over medium-low heat. Add the flour and whisk until a smooth paste forms and begins to bubble. Continue to cook, whisking constantly, for 1 minute. Whisk in the milk and cook, whisking, until the sauce thickens and comes to a simmer. Then whisk for 1 minute more. Be sure to use the whisk to reach into the edges of the pan to keep the sauce from sticking and burning.

Reduce the heat to low and whisk in the mustard, paprika, caraway seeds (if using), and Tabasco sauce. Add the cheese all at once and stir with a large wooden spoon until it melts. Season with salt and pepper. Add the cooked macaroni and stir until it is well coated.

Pour the mixture into the prepared casserole and sprinkle the top with the bread crumbs. Bake for 30 minutes, or until the casserole is bubbly and the top is lightly browned. Remove the casserole from the oven and allow it to cool at least 10 minutes before serving.

Note: Leftover macaroni and cheese can be reheated, covered with foil, in a 300°F oven for 15 to 20 minutes.

3 tablespoons unsalted butter, plus additional for the casserole

3 tablespoons all-purpose flour

3 cups whole milk, warmed

¼ cup Sun-Dried Tomato Mustard or your favorite flavored mustard

1 teaspoon sweet paprika

1 teaspoon caraway seeds, optional

3 dashes Tabasco sauce

¼ pound Swiss, shredded

¼ pound Gouda, shredded

¼ pound Cheddar, shredded

Salt and freshly ground black pepper to taste

4 cups elbow macaroni, cooked according to the package directions and drained

2 tablespoons unflavored dried bread crumbs

MAKES 6 TO 8 SERVINGS

Thai Peanut Noodle Salad

With a bottle of Roasted Garlic Peanut Sauce in your pantry, this vegetarian dish can be put together in no time. Add a cup or two of sliced cooked chicken, leftover sliced steak, or cooked shrimp as you wish.

Combine the scallions, bell peppers, cucumber, peanuts, and peanut sauce in a large bowl. Add the pasta and toss until everything is well combined. Sprinkle with the cilantro and serve. The pasta can be refrigerated and served chilled if desired; it will keep for 2 days covered in the refrigerator.

2 scallions, thinly sliced

1 red bell pepper, cored, seeded, and julienned

1 yellow bell pepper, cored, seeded, and julienned

1 small cucumber, quartered, seeded, and julienned into 2-inch pieces

½ cup finely chopped dry-roasted peanuts

1½ cups Roasted Garlic Peanut Sauce

1 pound linguine, cooked according to the package directions, rinsed in cold water, and drained

3 tablespoons finely chopped cilantro

MAKES 4 TO 6 SERVINGS

Penne with Fennel, Lemon, and Pine Nuts

Vegetable relish on pasta? It makes a nice change from marinara sauce. We use our Fresh Fennel Relish, but any other savory vegetable relish will work, as will chopped marinated artichokes, which we suggest here as an alternative.

Place the lemons in a small saucepan and add enough water so they float at least 2 inches above the bottom of the pan. Cover the pan, place it over high heat, and bring the water to a boil. Lower the heat to medium and simmer until the lemons are tender when pierced with a knife, about 40 minutes. Drain the lemons and allow them to cool completely.

Cut the lemons in half and scoop out the centers using a spoon; discard the pulp. Scrape out all the white pith from the lemon halves, leaving only the softened rind. Slice the rind into thin slivers and set aside. You can prepare the lemon rinds up to 8 hours in advance; keep them covered in the refrigerator.

Toast the nuts in a medium skillet over high heat, shaking the pan or gently stirring the nuts, until they are lightly golden, about 3 minutes. (If they start to burn around the edges, lower the heat to medium.) Remove the nuts from the pan to stop them from cooking and set aside.

Bring 4 quarts salted water to a boil in a large stockpot over high heat. Add the penne, bring the water back to a boil, and cook until the pasta is tender, 8 to 10 minutes. Drain.

Place the penne in a large mixing bowl, add the olive oil, and toss until the pasta is well coated. Add the lemon rind, nuts, relish, and parsley, and stir until well combined. Season with salt and pepper.

Serve the pasta warm or cold. The pasta will keep for up to 3 days tightly covered in the refrigerator.

3 lemons

1 cup pine nuts

1 pound dried penne

3 tablespoons extra virgin olive oil

1½ cups Fresh Fennel Relish or chopped marinated artichoke hearts

¼ cup finely chopped flat-leaf parsley

Salt and freshly ground pepper to taste

MAKES 8 SERVINGS

Smoked Trout Salad with Cranberry Horseradish Vinaigrette

Smoked trout has a bold flavor, so we serve it with a vinaigrette flavored with a touch of our Cranberry Horseradish Sauce. Smoked sturgeon, tuna, and bluefish are good alternatives. For a sit-down first course, serve a trio of smoked fish: this salad, smoked scallops with a fruit chutney, and smoked salmon topped with crème fraîche.

TO PREPARE THE VINAIGRETTE

Combine the oil, horseradish sauce, vinegar, and orange juice in a blender. Pulse on and off until the mixture blends easily, then blend until smooth. Season with salt and pepper. Set aside. The vinaigrette can be made up to 2 days ahead and kept refrigerated, covered. Bring it to room temperature and blend for 10 seconds to remulsify before serving.

TO ASSEMBLE THE SALAD

Cut the rind from the orange using a sharp knife and remove all the white pith. Cut down along the membranes to release the individual sections.

Place the lettuce leaves on a large platter. Top with the watercress, trout, orange, and red onion, in that order. Drizzle ½ cup of the vinaigrette over the salad and sprinkle with the parsley. Serve immediately, with the remaining vinaigrette on the side.

For the vinaigrette

- ½ cup extra virgin olive oil
- 6 tablespoons Cranberry Horseradish Sauce or 5 tablespoons whole-berry cranberry sauce plus 1 tablespoon jarred horseradish
- 2 tablespoons cider vinegar
- 2 tablespoons fresh orange juice
- Salt and freshly ground black pepper to taste

For the salad

- 1 large navel orange
- 12 large green-leaf lettuce leaves
- 1 small bunch watercress, thick stems removed
- 2 large smoked trout fillets (about 1 pound), broken into 1-inch pieces
- ½ small red onion, thinly sliced
- 1 tablespoon minced flat-leaf parsley

MAKES 4 SERVINGS

Wild Rice Salad with Shrimp

Wild rice has a chewier texture than white rice, and it takes longer to cook, about 45 minutes to an hour. In this recipe, the nuts add crunch, the vegetables add color, and our Lemon Peppercorn Vinaigrette ties all the flavors together.

Rub the spice mixture into the shrimp.

Heat the oil in a medium skillet over high heat until hot but not smoking. Add the shrimp all at once and cook, stirring constantly, until pink and firm, about 3 minutes. Transfer the shrimp to a large mixing bowl.

Add the pecans to the pan, lower the heat to medium, and cook the pecans, tossing occasionally, until they smell nutty and are lightly toasted, about 1 minute. Add the pecans to the bowl with the shrimp. Allow them to cool.

Add the rice, scallions, bell pepper, tomatoes, cranberries, parsley, thyme, vinaigrette, and salt and pepper to the shrimp and nuts and toss until well mixed. Cover the salad and refrigerate until ready to serve. The salad keeps well for up to 3 days.

1 tablespoon Spice Rub for Seafood or your favorite spice mixture

¾ pound medium shrimp (about 24), shelled and deveined

3 tablespoons extra virgin olive oil

¾ cup pecan pieces

3 cups cooked wild rice (follow the package instructions), cooled

2 scallions, thinly sliced

1 red bell pepper, cored, seeded, and diced

6 cherry tomatoes, halved

½ cup dried cranberries

½ cup finely chopped flat-leaf parsley

1 tablespoon thyme leaves

½ cup Lemon Peppercorn Vinaigrette or your favorite vinaigrette

Salt and freshly ground black pepper to taste

MAKES 6 TO 8 SERVINGS

Endive, Apple, and Walnut Salad

In early fall, apple trees are heavy with fruit, and pick-your-own orchards are open all through Maine. We pick crisp apples like Mutzu, Cortland, Northern Spy, or even Granny Smiths for this salad. Their crunchy texture and tartness balance the rich cheese. Serve this salad with plenty of bread and a bottle of dry white wine or sparkling cider.

Combine the endives, apples, and walnuts in a large mixing bowl. Add the vinaigrette and toss until well coated. Season with salt and pepper.

Place the romaine on a large platter. Top with the radicchio, leaving a visible green border all the way around. Spoon the endive-apple mixture onto the center of the platter and scatter the cheese over it. Serve immediately.

4 Belgian endives, halved and thinly sliced

3 large tart apples, cored, halved, and thinly sliced

1 cup walnut halves

½ cup Roasted Garlic Vinaigrette or your favorite vinaigrette

Salt and freshly ground black pepper to taste

16 large romaine lettuce leaves

12 large radicchio leaves

¼ pound Asiago or other sharp hard cheese, shaved or thinly sliced

MAKES 4 SERVINGS

Seared Tuna Salade Niçoise

This Mediterranean classic is traditionally made with canned tuna and fresh tomatoes, but our version includes fresh tuna and Marinated Sun-Dried Tomatoes. Arrange the salad on a large serving platter so guests can help themselves.

Bring 4 quarts salted water to a boil in a large pan over high heat. Add the green beans and cook for 2 minutes. Remove the beans with a small strainer or slotted spoon and set them aside to cool. Add the potatoes to the water and bring the water back to a boil. Reduce the heat to medium and boil the potatoes until they are just tender when pierced with the tip of a knife, about 20 minutes. Drain the potatoes in a colander and set them aside to cool.

Rub the tuna with 1 tablespoon of the olive oil and season with salt and pepper. Place a skillet over high heat for 2 minutes. Add the remaining 1 tablespoon oil to the skillet and tilt the pan to coat the bottom. Add the tuna and sear it for 1 minute. Turn and sear the other side for 1 minute. (If you like your tuna more thoroughly cooked, sear it for 2 to 4 minutes per side.) Remove the tuna from the pan and set it aside to cool.

Arrange the lettuce on a large decorative platter. Distribute the potatoes, green beans, and bell peppers evenly over the lettuce. Separate the red onion slices into rings and scatter them over the vegetables. Top with the sun-dried tomatoes. Place the hard-boiled eggs and olives around the edge of the platter. Cut the tuna into ½-inch slices and place them over the salad, overlapping them slightly. Garnish the platter with the basil leaves.

Serve the vinaigrette on the side.

The salad can be assembled ahead and kept covered with plastic in the refrigerator for up to 2 hours.

½ pound small green beans

1½ pounds small new potatoes

1½ pounds sushi-quality tuna

2 tablespoons extra virgin olive oil

Salt and freshly ground black pepper to taste

2 small heads green-leaf lettuce, leaves separated, washed, and dried

1 red bell pepper, cored, seeded, and julienned

1 yellow bell pepper, cored, seeded, and julienned

1 small red onion, thinly sliced into rings

½ cup Marinated Sun-Dried Tomatoes, drained and roughly chopped

3 hard-boiled eggs, peeled and quartered

16 large black olives

10 to 12 fresh basil leaves

1 cup Roasted Garlic Vinaigrette or your favorite vinaigrette

MAKES 4 TO 6 SERVINGS

Lobster Tabbouleh Salad

Tabbouleh is a traditional Middle Eastern salad made from bulgur wheat, tomatoes, onions, parsley, and mint. In our store kitchens, we add some cooked lobster and dress it with Roasted Red Pepper Vinaigrette.

Place the bulgur wheat in a large mixing bowl and cover with 1 cup boiling water. Let sit for 30 minutes or until the water is completely absorbed.

Fluff the bulgur with a fork. Add the tomatoes, cucumber, onion, parsley, mint, lobster, vinaigrette, and salt and pepper. Toss until well combined.

Cover the salad tightly and refrigerate for at least 4 hours, or overnight, before serving. The salad will keep for up to 2 days.

1 cup medium-fine
    bulgur wheat

1 cup finely chopped
    seeded tomatoes

1 medium cucumber,
    peeled, seeded, and
    finely chopped

1 cup finely chopped
    red onion

¼ cup finely chopped
    flat-leaf parsley

¼ cup finely chopped
    mint

1½ cups (about ¾
    pound) roughly
    chopped cooked
    lobster meat
    (see page 10)

¼ cup plus 2 table-
    spoons Roasted Red
    Pepper Vinaigrette or
    your favorite vinai-
    grette

Salt and freshly ground
    black pepper to taste

MAKES 4 TO 6 SERVINGS

Seafood

Lobstering is big business in Maine. Drive along the coast, from the Piscataqua River all the way up to Calais, and you'll see lobster pounds lining the roads, and lobster boats going in or out of nearly every port. Nothing much has changed since Maine author Sarah Orne Jewett described such a scene in *The Country of the Pointed Firs* in 1899.

But lobster isn't the only seafood we enjoy. Mussels, clams, salmon, scrod, and scallops are on nearly every menu from the Cape Neddick Inn, a sophisticated restaurant in York, to the Fisherman's Friend, a diner in Stonington. And while salsa and ketchup may be the favorite condiments in the rest of America, cocktail sauce is the most common one in Maine. Our Lemon Dill Cocktail Sauce is the perfect accompaniment to a steamed lobster or a pound of shrimp. In these recipes we show you how our condiments can add flavor to many seafood dishes. Steaming mussels in white wine with Maine Maple Champagne Mustard highlights their natural sweetness. Melted Pineapple Mint Jam, with a little butter and minced shallots, makes a quick, rich sauce for sautéed scallops. From crab cakes to salmon fillets, swordfish to sea bass, any seafood can benefit from the variety found in today's pantry.

Roasted Lobster

Roasted Lobster

Maine lobster meat is sweet to begin with, and roasting the lobsters at a high temperature makes them even sweeter. You can even smell them while they're cooking—it's a mouthwatering aroma indigenous to Maine. Some folks slather the lobsters with butter before roasting them, but butter on its own will burn at high heat. We use a combination of Roasted Garlic Oil and butter, so the lobsters won't burn.

Bring a large deep pot of salted water to a boil. Plunge the lobsters headfirst into the boiling water, and cook until they stop moving and just start to turn red, about 2 minutes. Meanwhile, fill a large bowl with ice water. Remove the lobsters from the hot water with long tongs and place them in the ice water. Allow them to cool completely.

Remove the lobsters from the water and drain on paper towels. You can prepare the lobsters to this point up to 4 hours ahead and keep them tightly covered in the refrigerator.

Preheat the oven to 500°F.

Place the lobsters belly side down on a cutting board. Split the lobsters in half: Using a sharp heavy knife, cut into the shell just behind the head, with the blade toward the eyes, and cut all the way through the head. Turn the lobsters around and extend the cuts back all the way through the tail.

Place the lobsters shell side down in a roasting pan or on a baking sheet large enough to hold them in one layer. Combine the oil and melted butter in a small bowl, and brush the lobsters with half of this mixture. Bake for 20 minutes, brushing with the remaining oil and butter halfway through.

Season with salt and pepper. Serve immediately.

Two 1½-pound live lobsters

½ cup Roasted Garlic Oil or olive oil

2 tablespoons unsalted butter, melted

Salt and freshly ground black pepper to taste

MAKES 2 SERVINGS

Sesame-Seared Salmon with Lingonberry Jam

Michele Duval, owner and chef of the Cape Neddick Inn in Maine, developed this recipe using one of our favorite preserves and rich-fleshed salmon, to balance the sweetness of the jam. For the freshest fillets, have your fishmonger slice them from a side of salmon, rather than buying precut portions.

TO PREPARE THE SAUCE

Pour the oil into a medium saucepan set over medium heat. Add the onion and cook, stirring occasionally, until translucent, about 5 minutes. Add the spice rub and cook for 30 seconds, stirring constantly. Reduce the heat to low, add the jam, and stir until it is completely melted. Add the rice wine and balsamic vinegars, raise the heat to medium, and bring to a boil. Cook for 30 seconds, stirring constantly to avoid burning the sauce. Immediately pour the sauce into a small bowl and cover to keep warm. The sauce can be made up to 1 week ahead of time and kept tightly covered in the refrigerator. Reheat in a small pan before serving.

TO PREPARE THE SALMON

Rub the top of each salmon fillet with ½ teaspoon of the sesame oil and sprinkle with the sesame seeds.

Place a skillet large enough to hold the fish in one layer without crowding over medium heat. (If necessary, use two skillets.) Add the peanut oil to the pan and heat the oil until is hot but not smoking. Add the salmon skin side up to the pan and cook for 4 minutes. Turn the salmon over and cook for another 4 minutes.

Transfer the salmon to a serving platter or individual plates and spoon or brush 1½ tablespoons of the sauce over each fillet. Serve immediately, with the remaining sauce on the side.

For the sauce

1 tablespoon extra virgin olive oil

1 medium yellow onion, finely chopped

1 tablespoon Spice Rub for Seafood or your favorite spice mixture

½ cup Lingonberry Jam or raspberry jam

¼ cup rice wine vinegar

1 tablespoon balsamic vinegar

For the salmon

Four 8-ounce center cut salmon fillets, about 1½ inches thick, skin left on

2 tablespoons toasted sesame oil

2 tablespoons *each* black and white sesame seeds, tossed

2 tablespoons peanut oil or vegetable oil

MAKES 4 SERVINGS

Pan-Seared Scallops with Roasted Sweet Potatoes

One of the reasons our preserves are so versatile is because we combine so many herbs and spices with fruit—ginger and peach, sage and black-berry, chipotle and cherry, to name a few. When the first jar of Pineapple Mint Jam came out of our test kitchen, we started cooking with it immediately, coming up with ideas like this one, before it even went on sale.

Preheat the oven to 400°F.

Cut the sweet potato into six slices, discarding the ends. Rub the slices with 1 tablespoon of the olive oil, place them in a small roasting pan just large enough to hold them in one layer, and sprinkle lightly with salt and pepper.

Roast the potato slices until tender, about 30 minutes, turning them once halfway through. Set the potatoes aside and cover to keep warm while you prepare the scallops.

Heat a skillet pan over medium heat for 1 minute. Add the remaining 1 table-spoon olive oil and the butter. When the butter is foaming, add the scallops and cook for 2 minutes on each side, or until they feel firm to the touch and are lightly browned. Remove the scallops from the pan with tongs and set them aside.

Add the shallots to the pan and sauté until softened, about 3 minutes. Add the vermouth and scrape up any brown bits that are stuck to the bottom of the pan. Let the vermouth boil for 30 seconds, reducing and thickening slightly. Add the jam and stir until it's completely melted and incorporated into the sauce. Stir in the cider vinegar and season with salt and pepper.

1 large sweet potato, peeled

2 tablespoons extra virgin olive oil

Salt and freshly ground black pepper to taste

1 tablespoon unsalted butter

8 large sea scallops, about ¾ pound

3 tablespoons finely chopped shallots

2 tablespoons white vermouth

2 tablespoons Pineapple Mint Jam or pineapple jam

1 teaspoon cider vinegar

2 mint sprigs

Place the scallops back in the pan and swirl them in the sauce to heat them through. Remove from the heat.

Place 3 slices of potato in the center of each plate, overlapping them slightly. Place the scallops on top of the potatoes and spoon the sauce over them. Garnish with the mint sprigs and serve immediately.

MAKES 2 SERVINGS

Swordfish Kebabs with Toasted Basmati-Orzo Pilaf

Swordfish is perfect for skewering because its meaty texture doesn't flake when cooked. This hearty cold-water fish is flavored with our Spice Rub and served over basmati rice: a long-grain white rice with a light flowery fragrance. We added orzo, a slightly chewy, rice-shaped pasta, for additional texture.

Place the swordfish in a medium bowl. Add 3 tablespoons of the olive oil, the lemon zest, lemon juice, and spice rub and toss until the fish is well coated.

Skewer the fish on the bamboo skewers, placing the same number of pieces on each. Cover with plastic wrap and refrigerate for up to 2 hours.

About 20 minutes before serving, melt the butter in a medium saucepan over medium-high heat. Add the rice and orzo and stir constantly until they begin to turn a light golden brown. Add about two-thirds of the scallions and the chicken stock. Bring to a boil, stirring often to make sure the rice and pasta do not stick to the bottom of the pan. Reduce the heat to low, cover, and simmer for 12 minutes. Turn off the heat and allow the pilaf to rest while you prepare the fish.

Heat a skillet large enough to hold the skewers in one layer over high heat for 1 minute. Add the remaining olive oil; the oil should ripple from the heat of the pan. Swirl the pan to coat the entire bottom with the oil, then immediately add the fish kebabs and cook for 2 minutes on all sides, or until the fish is just cooked through.

Fluff the pilaf with a fork and season with salt and pepper. Divide the pilaf among six plates and top each with a swordfish kebab. Sprinkle with the remaining scallions and serve immediately, with the chutney on the side.

3 pounds swordfish steaks, about 1½ inches thick, cut into 1½-inch cubes

¼ cup plus 1 tablespoon extra virgin olive oil

1 tablespoon grated lemon zest

Juice of 1 lemon

1 tablespoon Spice Rub for Seafood or your favorite spice mixture

2 tablespoons unsalted butter

1 cup basmati rice

1 cup orzo

2 scallions, thinly sliced

1 quart chicken stock or canned low-sodium broth

Salt and freshly ground black pepper to taste

2 cups Old Farmhouse Chutney or fruit chutney

Six 8-inch bamboo skewers, soaked in water for 20 minutes

MAKES 6 SERVINGS

Seafood Pot Pie

Just down the road from our store in York, Maine, is Finest Kind, one of our favorite fish markets. Locals know it's where to find some of the freshest seafood in York, and tourists stop to purchase live lobsters packed to travel. You can't miss it; the parking lot is always full. We prepare this elegant dish with whatever catches our eyes when we stop by after work, but shrimp and scallops, which are always available, are essential. We also like scrod, but halibut or snapper are fine substitutes.

Preheat the oven to 425°F.

Melt the butter in a medium saucepan over medium-low heat. Add the onion and cook, stirring constantly, until softened, about 10 minutes.

Whisk the flour into the butter and onion mixture until the flour is completely incorporated and the mixture is bubbling. Cook, whisking, for 30 seconds so the flour will lose its raw taste; it should not turn brown. Slowly whisk in the milk. Raise the heat to medium and continue to whisk until the sauce thickens and bubbles. Reach into the corners of the pan with the whisk to prevent the sauce from sticking. Reduce the heat to low and whisk in the vermouth. Bring the sauce back to a simmer, then remove the pan from the heat.

Squeeze the excess water from the spinach with your hands. Add the spinach to the sauce, breaking up any clumps. Add the mustard, nutmeg, and salt and pepper and whisk until the sauce is smooth. Cover to keep warm.

Combine the spice rub and 2 quarts water in a large saucepan. Bring the water to a boil over high heat. Add the shrimp, scallops, and scrod, and reduce the heat to medium and cook for 3 minutes, or until the shrimp are pink, the scallops firm, and the scrod opaque. Remove the seafood from the broth

Ingredients

6 tablespoons (¾ stick) unsalted butter

2 cups finely chopped onion

½ cup all-purpose flour

2 cups milk

1 cup white vermouth

Two 10-ounce packages frozen chopped spinach, thawed

½ cup plus 2 tablespoons Roasted Garlic Mustard or Dijon mustard

½ teaspoon ground nutmeg

Salt and freshly ground black pepper to taste

¼ cup Spice Rub for Seafood or your favorite spice mixture

½ pound medium shrimp, peeled and deveined

½ pound small bay scallops

using a slotted spoon and place it in the sauce. Gently stir with a large rubber spatula until the seafood is completely coated with sauce.

Spoon the mixture into a 6- to 8-cup gratin dish or shallow casserole. Sprinkle the top with the cheese. Cover the dish with the puff pastry, allowing it to overhang the sides of the dish by ¼ to ½ inch. (If the pastry dough is in small pieces, not large enough to cover the dish, overlap them as necessary.) Brush the top with the beaten egg, to give the finished pot pie a shiny golden color.

Bake for 25 minutes, or until the pastry is puffed and brown. Allow the casserole to rest for 10 minutes before serving.

1 pound scrod fillet, about 1 inch thick, cut into 1-inch cubes

1½ cups shredded Swiss (about 6 ounces)

One 1-pound package frozen puff pastry, thawed

1 large egg, beaten with 2 tablespoons water

MAKES 6 TO 8 SERVINGS

Red Pepper-Sesame Bass

Striped bass, a delicate fish, is steamed whole and then served with our Roasted Red Pepper Sesame Sauce on the side. When choosing a whole bass or any fish, look for clear eyes—the true measure of a fish's freshness. Alternatively, you can use a one-pound fish fillet or steak here, but you'll need to choose a thicker-fleshed fish, such as halibut or Chilean sea bass. You won't need to score the fish if the fillets are skinless.

Place a wire cooling rack in a deep roasting pan large enough to hold an oval platter or a large dinner plate. Add water to the pan to a depth of 1 inch. Cover the pan (use aluminum foil if necessary) and bring the water to a simmer over medium heat.

Meanwhile, rinse the fish in cold water and blot it dry with paper towels. Score the fish 2 times on each side with a sharp knife, just deep enough to cut through the skin; do not cut all the way to the bone. Rub the fish all over with the sesame oil and season with salt and pepper.

Spread the parsley on an oval platter or large dinner plate that will fit in the roasting pan. Lay the fish on the bed of parsley. If a little of the tail and some of the head hang off the ends of the platter, that's okay. Stuff the scallions into the belly of the fish.

Place the platter on the rack in the roasting pan and cover tightly (use foil if necessary). Raise the heat to high and steam the fish for 15 minutes, or until the meat flakes when pulled with a fork.

One 1½- to 2-pound striped bass, gutted and cleaned

2 teaspoons toasted sesame oil

Salt and freshly ground black pepper to taste

1 small bunch flat-leaf parsley

3 scallions, trimmed

1 cup Roasted Red Pepper Sesame Sauce or pureed jarred pimientos

1 teaspoon sesame seeds

Meanwhile, bring the roasted red pepper sesame sauce to a simmer in a small saucepan.

Transfer the fish to a clean serving platter, using two large spatulas. Pour the warm sauce around the fish and sprinkle the entire platter with the sesame seeds. Serve immediately. Use two forks to gently remove the meat from the bones, and serve with crusty bread to soak up the sauce.

MAKES 2 SERVINGS

Crab Cakes

Good crab cakes are nothing more than lump crabmeat, seasonings, and cracker crunbs, held together with mayonnaise. Some folks add sautéed onions and celery. Others add eggs. Here's our favorite version.

Heat 1 tablespoon of the oil in a large skillet over medium heat. Add the celery and onion and cook until the vegetables are translucent and begining to soften, about 3 minutes. Transfer to a large mixing bowl. Set the skillet aside.

Add the mayonnaise, ⅓ cup of the cracker crumbs, the mustard, and egg to the onion and celery and mix until thoroughly combined. Add the crabmeat and pepper, gently folding in the crab just until it is incorporated. (Overmixing will cause the crab to break up into tiny shreds; the crab cakes will still be delicious, but they will have a smoother texture with fewer lumps of crab.)

Put the remaining 1 cup cracker crumbs in a shallow dish. Shape ¼ cup of the crab mixture into a patty, lay it in the cracker crumbs, and sprinkle the crumbs all around to cover the entire patty. Pick it up, compacting the patty between your palms to help the crumbs adhere and the mixture hold its shape, and place on a plate. Repeat with the remaining crab mixture.

Heat 1 tablespoon of the remaining oil and 1 tablespoon of the butter in the skillet used for the onion and celery over medium heat until the butter melts and foams. Add as many crab cakes to the pan as will fit without crowding and cook for 3 minutes on each side, or until golden brown. Transfer to a plate. Repeat with the remaining cakes, adding more butter and oil to the pan as necessary to keep them from sticking.

Serve the crab cakes hot, with the mango mayonnaise.

About 3 tablespoons extra virgin olive oil

½ cup minced celery

½ cup minced onion

⅓ cup mayonnaise

1⅓ cups salty cracker crumbs (preferably saltines)

2 tablespoons Lemon Peppercorn Mustard or Dijon mustard

1 large egg, lightly beaten

1 pound lump crabmeat, picked over for shells and cartilage

Freshly ground black pepper to taste

About 2 tablespoons unsalted butter

1¼ cups Curried Mango Mayonnaise (recipe follows) or tartar sauce

MAKES 12 SMALL CRAB CAKES

Curried Mango Mayonnaise

Combine the mayonnaise, mango sauce, and Tabasco in a small bowl, mixing until thoroughly combined. Cover and refrigerate until ready to use. The mayonnaise can be made up to 2 days ahead of time.

1 cup mayonnaise

½ cup Curried Mango Grill Sauce

4 dashes Tabasco sauce

MAKES 1½ CUPS

Steamed Mussels

Jonathan's brother, Gregory, the talented chef of Gregory's Restaurant in Greenland, New Hampshire, created this dish when he taught a class in one of our stores. The mussels are steamed in olive oil, wine, and our Maple Champagne Mustard. Serve plenty of crusty bread to soak up every drop of the sauce.

Discard any mussels with broken shells.

Pour the olive oil into a saucepan or skillet large enough to hold the mussels and still give you room to toss them around a bit. Heat the oil over high heat until it is rippling. Add the mussels all at once and toss to coat them with the oil. Add the garlic, shallots, and horseradish and cook for 3 minutes, tossing and stirring the mussels with one or two long wooden spoons.

Add the mustard, lemon juice, butter, and wine to the pan, toss well, and bring to a boil. Cover and allow the mussels to steam for 1 minute or until they open.

Transfer the mussels to a large deep serving bowl (discarding any that did not open) and pour the sauce from the pan over them. Sprinkle with the parsley and serve immediately.

6 pounds mussels, scrubbed and debearded

¼ cup extra virgin olive oil

2 tablespoons finely chopped garlic

3 tablespoons chopped shallots

1 tablespoon jarred white horseradish

2 tablespoons Maine Maple Champagne Mustard or honey mustard

¼ cup fresh lemon juice

6 tablespoons (¾ stick) unsalted butter, at room temperature

½ cup dry white wine or clam juice

1 tablespoon finely chopped flat-leaf parsley

MAKES 4 SERVINGS

Meat

Visitors to Maine (or people "from away," as we call them) are surprised at how much meat we eat up here. True, seafood is plentiful, but much of Maine extends hundreds of miles inland from the ocean. Turn west off the coastal road, U.S. Route 1, and it's just a short while before the lobster pounds are replaced by chicken coops and cattle farms.

You need a little something besides ketchup and mayonnaise to top all of those grilled chicken sandwiches and hamburgers. In the dead of winter, try roasting a ham, basted with brown sugar, spicy chutney, and a hearty flavored mustard. Or rub herb-flavored butter over a chicken and baste it with melted blackberry or blueberry jam as it cooks. It's contemporary comfort food, Maine-style.

In summer, like most people, we don't want our ovens going full blast, so we've created several meat dishes that don't need to cook for hours. When we add a boost of flavor from the pantry, they're just as comforting as their winter counterparts. A quick chicken stir-fry spiked with Tomato Ginger Jam is perfect at the end of a hot August day, and Lemon Pear Grilled Chicken is just right after a hard day at the beach.

When you taste what a wide variety of condiments can do for meat, you'll know why we sometimes say "no" to lobster, even in Maine.

Lemon Pear Grilled Chicken

This chicken dish gets its intense flavor from our Lemon Pear Marmalade. Start marinating the chicken the day before, if you can, so it has plenty of time to absorb the flavor of the marinade. Although the chicken is great hot, we think the flavor is even better after it's cooled, making it great for picnics, brown-bag lunches, or late-night snacks.

Combine the marmalade, lemon juice, vinegar, and oil in a large bowl. Whisk until the marmalade dissolves. Season with salt and pepper. Add the chicken pieces and toss to coat completely. Cover and place in the refrigerator for at least 4 hours, or overnight, turning the chicken in the marinade once or twice.

Prepare an outdoor grill or preheat the broiler.

Remove the chicken from the marinade, reserving the marinade, and place it skin side up on the grill or skin side down in a pan under the broiler. Cook for 10 minutes, basting with the marinade once or twice. Turn the chicken over and cook for another 10 minutes, basting once or twice. Continue to cook the chicken, turning the pieces and basting them with the marinade once or twice for 10 minutes more, or until an instant-read thermometer registers 185°F when stuck into the thickest part of the thigh. The juices should run clear, not pink or red.

Serve the chicken hot, at room temperature, or cold. The chicken will keep covered in the refrigerator for up to 3 days.

1 cup Lemon Pear Marmalade or lemon marmalade

¾ cup fresh lemon juice

¼ cup cider vinegar

¼ cup extra virgin olive oil

Salt and freshly ground black pepper to taste

2 chickens (about 3 pounds each), cut into serving pieces, excess fat removed

MAKES 4 TO 6 SERVINGS

Blackberry Sage Roast Chicken

When you live in a place where the winters are long and cold, you learn the trick of making quick, hearty dinners. Sure, anyone can roast a chicken. But it doesn't take much effort to add our sweet, herbal Blackberry Sage Tea Jam. What you'll get is a roast chicken that will warm you to the bone—and make an ordinary weeknight supper extraordinary.

TO PREPARE THE GLAZE

Combine the jam, vermouth, lemon juice, honey, and Worcestershire in a small saucepan. Place over medium heat and stir until the jam is completely melted. Raise the heat to high and boil the glaze for 1 minute. Remove from the heat and set the pan aside.

TO PREPARE THE CHICKEN

Preheat the oven to 350°F. Place a rack in a roasting pan large enough to hold the chicken comfortably.

Combine the butter, sage, and salt and pepper in a small bowl and mix until the sage is well incorporated into the butter.

Remove the giblets from the chicken and rinse the chicken inside and out. Remove any excess fat and pat the chicken dry. Starting at the neck, push your fingers in between the chicken skin and breast meat to create pockets for the butter. Stuff the herbed butter under the skin, then press the outside of the skin with your hands to spread the butter evenly.

Place the chicken breast side down on the rack in the pan and roast for 30 minutes. Turn the chicken breast side up and roast for 30 minutes more. Begin basting the chicken every 10 minutes with the glaze and continue to roast for a total 1½ hours, or until an instant-read meat thermometer reg-

For the glaze

½ cup Blackberry Sage Tea Jam, Boysenberry Jam, or blackberry jam

¼ cup white vermouth or dry white wine

1½ tablespoons fresh lemon juice, strained

1½ tablespoons honey

1½ teaspoons Worcestershire sauce

For the chicken

3 tablespoons unsalted butter, at room temperature

8 sage leaves, minced

Salt and freshly ground black pepper to taste

1 large roasting chicken (5 to 6 pounds)

isters 185°F when inserted into the thickest part of the thigh and the juices run clear.

Remove the chicken from the oven and cover it with foil to keep warm while you make the sauce.

TO PREPARE THE SAUCE

Skim the fat from the pan juices. Pour the stock into the roasting pan and, using a wooden spoon, scrape up any brown bits that are stuck to the bottom of the pan. Pour the pan juices and stock into the saucepan with the remaining glaze. Bring the mixture to a boil over high heat. Reduce the heat to low and simmer for 1 minute. Add the butter a few teaspoons at a time, whisking until the sauce thickens slightly. Season with salt and pepper. Turn off the heat and cover to keep the sauce warm while you carve the chicken.

Serve the chicken with the sauce on the side.

For the sauce

½ cup chicken stock or canned low-sodium broth

1 to 2 tablespoons unsalted butter, at room temperature

Salt and freshly ground black pepper to taste

MAKES 4 SERVINGS

Stir-fried Tomato Ginger Chicken

After years of eating the same dishes from our local Chinese takeout, we bought ourselves a wok. It's easy and the food is always hot when we eat it. This is our favorite, a sweet and tangy stir-fry that combines a few fresh ingredients with jam, that secret ingredient from our pantry. This throw-it-together-in-a-minute dish satisfies our hunger and our desire for a fast, flavorful meal. Serve this with steamed white rice.

Place a wok or large skillet over high heat for 1 minute. Add 1 tablespoon of the oil and swirl the pan to coat the bottom with oil. Add the chicken and cook, stirring constantly, until the chicken begins to brown, about 5 minutes. Transfer the chicken to a bowl and set it aside.

Lower the heat to medium and add the remaining 1 tablespoon oil to the hot pan. Add the bell peppers and garlic and cook over medium heat, stirring constantly, until the peppers begin to soften, about 2 minutes. Add the soy sauce, vermouth, jam, and pepper flakes and cook, stirring constantly, until the jam melts completely. Place the chicken back into the pan and stir until it's coated with sauce and everything is bubbling wildly. Season with salt and pepper.

Add the arrowroot, stirring until the sauce is thickened. Add the cilantro and toss until it is well distributed. Serve immediately.

2 tablespoons Roasted Garlic Oil

4 skinless, boneless chicken breasts, sliced into ¼-inch strips

2 small red bell peppers, cored, seeded, and julienned

2 large garlic cloves, minced

2 tablespoons soy sauce

1 tablespoon white vermouth or dry sherry

¼ cup Tomato Ginger Jam, Ginger Peach Tea Jam, or peach jam

½ teaspoon crushed red pepper flakes or to taste

Salt and freshly ground black pepper to taste

1 teaspoon arrowroot, dissolved in 1 tablespoon water

¼ cup finely chopped cilantro

MAKES 4 SERVINGS

Flank Steak Fajitas

Texas is the home of fajitas, and Texans always use flank or hanger steak, but you can use sirloin or any other tender cut of beef. Our Maple Chipotle Grille Sauce creates a marinade that melds the best of Maine and Tex-Mex. Serve individual dishes of sliced jalapeños, shredded lettuce, diced tomatoes, grated Monterey Jack, sour cream, and guacamole alongside these fajitas. Your guests can then fill their tortillas with the meat and any combination of ingredients they choose.

TO PREPARE THE MARINADE

Combine the grill sauce, red wine, olive oil, soy sauce, and lime juice in a blender. Blend on high for 10 seconds, or until the ingredients are well blended and emulsified.

Put the flank steak in a shallow baking dish and pour the marinade over it. Cover and refrigerate for at least 6 hours or overnight.

TO PREPARE THE FAJITAS

Prepare an outdoor grill or preheat the broiler. If possible, adjust the cooking surface of your grill or the broiler rack so that it sits 4 to 5 inches from the heat source.

While the coals heat, pour the oil into a medium skillet set over medium-low heat. Add the onions and peppers and cook, stirring occasionally, until the vegetables have softened, about 10 minutes. Stir in the cilantro and remove the pan from the heat. Cover to keep the vegetables warm.

Wrap the tortillas in aluminum foil and place them on the grill as far to one side as possible, to warm them up without drying them out. Turn the packet over once or twice while you cook the steak. Or, if you are using the broiler,

For the marinade

¾ cup Maple Chipotle Grille Sauce or spicy barbecue sauce

½ cup dry red wine

¼ cup extra virgin olive oil

¼ cup soy sauce

Juice of 1 lime

For the fajitas

One 2-pound flank steak, trimmed of excess fat

2 tablespoons Roasted Garlic Oil or olive oil

2 large white onions, cut into ½-inch rings

2 green bell peppers, cored, seeded, and cut into ½-inch strips

¼ cup finely chopped cilantro

8 large flour tortillas

place the packet of tortillas on a lower rack in the oven, where they will warm up from the heat of the broiler.

Remove the steak from the marinade, reserving the marinade, and place it on the grill or under the broiler. Cook for 5 minutes on each side for medium-rare, 6 minutes per side for medium, or 7 minutes per side for well-done, basting the steak with the marinade every 2 or 3 minutes. Remove the steak from the heat and allow it to rest for 5 minutes before slicing.

Cut the meat into thin slices, cutting on a sharp angle against the grain. Serve hot, with the tortillas and sautéed onions and peppers.

MAKES 4 SERVINGS

Spareribs with Vidalia Onion Fig Sauce

Onions and figs with ribs may sound a bit exotic, but it's actually the perfect combination because the natural sugar in the figs and onions caramelizes into a coating that imparts a wonderful flavor to the succulent pork. Long, slow baking creates the most tender ribs. You can finish them off on the grill for a smoky taste, but we just use the broiler and add a little liquid smoke to the sauce for a barbecued taste without the mess of charcoal.

Preheat the oven to 400°F.

Place the ribs in a large roasting pan and cover tightly with aluminum foil. Bake for 1½ hours, or until the ribs are tender but not falling off the bone.

While the ribs bake, combine the fig sauce, ketchup, vinegar, liquid smoke, Worcestershire, mustard, and red pepper flakes in a small saucepan. Stir until well combined. Set the pan over low heat, bring the sauce to a simmer, and simmer for 15 minutes, stirring occasionally. Season with salt and pepper. Set the pan aside.

When the ribs are tender, turn the oven to broil. Place the ribs on a broiler pan, meat side down. Spoon one-third of the sauce over the ribs and broil for 5 minutes. Turn the ribs over, and spoon another one-third of the sauce over them. Broil for 5 more minutes.

Place the ribs on a carving board and slice in between the bones. Serve immediately, with the remaining sauce on the side.

2 racks pork spareribs (about 3 pounds each)

1½ cups Vidalia Onion Fig Sauce or fruit-flavored barbecue sauce

¼ cup ketchup

⅔ cup red wine vinegar

1 tablespoon liquid smoke

1 teaspoon Worcestershire sauce

½ teaspoon dry mustard

½ teaspoon crushed red pepper flakes, or to taste

Salt and freshly ground black pepper to taste

MAKES 4 SERVINGS

Rack of Lamb
with Mustard-Herb Crust

Mustard and garlic are classic with lamb, so what could be better—or easier—than this herbed crust made with our Roasted Garlic Mustard and fragrant Roasted Garlic Oil? The crust not only adds flavor to the lamb but also helps protect the tender meat from drying out in the oven. Ask your butcher to French the rack of lamb—removing all the meat and fat from the upper part of the bones, leaving only the succulent tenderloin at the bottom. Serve the racks whole for a dramatic presentation, then carve into single or double chops.

Preheat the oven to 450°F.

Place the bread crumbs and parsley on a large plate and toss until well combined. Season the lamb with salt and pepper. Set aside.

Pour the oil into a roasting pan large enough to hold both racks comfortably. Place the pan over medium heat until the oil is hot enough to give off a little smoke. Add the lamb and brown the meat on all sides, about 5 minutes. Remove from the heat.

Place the lamb on a cutting board or a plate. Spoon 1 heaping tablespoon of the mustard over the meaty side of each rack and spread the mustard to cover the meat evenly. Holding the lamb by the bones, roll the mustard-coated meat in the bread crumbs. Place the racks back in the roasting pan, positioning them so that the bones are up and curving toward each other.

Roast for 15 minutes or until an instant-read meat thermometer stuck into the thickest part of the meat registers 120°F for rare, 125°F for medium-rare, or 130°F for medium. Allow the lamb to rest for 10 minutes before carving.

2 tablespoons unseasoned dried bread crumbs

1 tablespoon finely chopped flat-leaf parsley

2 racks of lamb (1½ to 2 pounds each)

Salt and freshly ground black pepper to taste

2 tablespoons Roasted Garlic Oil or olive oil

2 heaping tablespoons Roasted Garlic Mustard or other strong flavored mustard

MAKES 4 SERVINGS

Moroccan Pork Tenderloins

Somewhat spicy, these pork tenderloins are best started the day before so they can marinate overnight in the traditional mix of Moroccan spices, including turmeric, cumin, cinnamon, and ginger, made even more exotic with our Sugar Plum Jam. You can cook the tenderloins right before serving, or broil them ahead and keep them tightly wrapped in the refrigerator. They'll reheat in 15 minutes, wrapped in foil, in a 350°F oven—or slice them cold and use them in sandwiches, topped with chutney.

Combine the jam, vinegar, oil, turmeric, cumin, cinnamon, ginger, salt, and pepper in a small bowl. Whisk until the jam is well combined with the spices.

Place the tenderloins in a baking pan just large enough to hold them. Pour the jam mixture over them. Cover and refrigerate for at least 4 hours, or overnight, turning the pork once or twice.

Preheat the broiler. If possible, adjust the rack so it sits 4 inches from the heat source and keep warm.

Prepare the couscous according to the package directions and set aside.

Remove the pork from the marinade, reserving the marinade, and place on the broiler pan. Broil for about 20 minutes, turning once and basting with the marinade every 3 to 5 minutes until an instant-read thermometer registers 165°F when inserted into the thickest part of the meat. Allow the pork to rest for 5 minutes before slicing.

Carve the pork on an angle into ¼- to ½-inch slices. Serve hot with the couscous, garnished with the sliced plums and almonds.

½ cup Sugar Plum Jam or plum jam

1 tablespoon balsamic vinegar

1 tablespoon extra virgin olive oil

1½ teaspoons ground turmeric

1 teaspoon ground cumin

½ teaspoon ground cinnamon

½ teaspoon ground ginger

1 teaspoon salt

½ teaspoon freshly ground black pepper

Two 1-pound pork tenderloins

One 10-ounce package couscous

2 red plums, pitted and thinly sliced

¼ cup sliced blanched almonds

MAKES 4 SERVINGS

Sunday Ham Dinner

Sunday evenings are times for families to gather. Our families traditionally shared a hearty ham dinner, complete with baked beans and corn bread. Today, we still make baked ham dinners, but we spice things up with chutney and mustard, both to coat the ham and make the beans tastier. A spiral-sliced ham makes serving this meal easy. If you can't find one at your local supermarket, you can order one directly from Stonewall Kitchen (see page 155). Make all three dishes in the order listed, or prepare the ham and the beans ahead and reheat them, uncovered, in a 350°F oven for 10 to 15 minutes while the corn bread cools.

Preheat the oven to 300°F.

Combine the brown sugar, mustard, chutney, and apple juice concentrate in a small bowl and mix with a wooden spoon until the glaze has the consistency of a thick sauce.

Place the ham in a large roasting pan and spread half the glaze all over it. Cover the ham loosely with aluminum foil and bake for 30 minutes. Uncover the ham and bake, basting with the remaining glaze every 5 to 7 minutes, for an additional 30 minutes, or until the glaze is browned and an instant-read thermometer stuck into the thickest part of the ham registers 140°F. (If you run out of glaze, baste the ham with the pan juices.)

Serve the ham or warm at room temperature. Any leftovers can be kept covered in the refrigerator for 3 to 4 days.

FOR THE BAKED BEANS

Preheat the oven to 350°F.

Place the beans in a 4-quart bean pot or casserole and set aside.

½ cup packed light brown sugar

⅓ cup Maple Champagne Mustard or honey mustard

⅓ cup Apple Cranberry Chutney or other fruit chutney

⅓ cup apple juice concentrate, thawed

One 6- to 8-pound smoked and spiral-sliced half ham

Baked Beans

Two 15½-ounce cans pinto beans, drained and rinsed

16 slices bacon, cut into ½-inch pieces

1 large green bell pepper, cored, seeded, and diced

1 large white onion, diced

2 tart apples, such as Granny Smith, peeled, seeded, and finely chopped

⅔ cup packed dark brown sugar

⅔ cup ketchup

Sauté the bacon in a large skillet over medium heat until crisp. Remove the bacon from the pan with a slotted spoon and add it to the beans.

Discard half the rendered fat from the skillet. Sauté the bell pepper and onion in the remaining bacon drippings over medium heat until the onion is translucent and the pepper is beginning to soften, about 5 minutes. Add the apples, brown sugar, ketchup, mustard, salt, garlic powder, pepper, and beer to the onion and pepper. Stir until the sugar dissolves and the mixture comes to a boil.

Pour the apple mixture into the pot with the beans and bacon. Mix until well combined.

Bake, uncovered, for 1 hour, or until the liquid is reduced to a thick sauce. Serve hot or warm.

FOR THE FARMHOUSE BUTTERMILK CORN BREAD

Preheat the oven to 425°F. Grease a 9-inch square baking pan.

Combine the cornmeal, flour, baking powder, salt, baking soda, and chili powder (if using) in a medium bowl. Whisk together until well blended.

Mix the buttermilk, eggs, melted butter, and corn in a large bowl until well combined. Stir in the dry ingredients and mix just until combined; do not overmix.

Spread the batter into the prepared pan and bake for 20 minutes, or until lightly browned on top. A toothpick inserted in the center should come out clean. Allow the bread to cool in the pan for at least 10 minutes before cutting. Serve hot or warm, with lots of butter.

⅔ cup Bourbon Molasses Mustard or honey mustard

2 teaspoons salt

1 teaspoon garlic powder

1 teaspoon freshly ground black pepper

Two 12-ounce bottles light or dark beer

Farmhouse Buttermilk Corn Bread

1 cup yellow cornmeal

¾ cup all-purpose flour

1 tablespoon baking powder

1 teaspoon salt

½ teaspoon baking soda

1 tablespoon chili powder, optional

1 cup buttermilk

2 large eggs

4 tablespoons (½ stick) unsalted butter, melted

1 cup fresh, canned, or thawed frozen corn kernels

MAKES 10 TO 12 SERVINGS

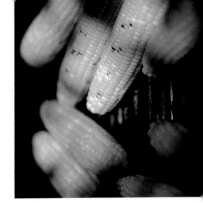

Vegetables
and Sides

In Maine, the growing season is short. The tomatoes aren't ready for harvest until mid-July. By mid-September, the vegetables are already in danger of frost, and all that's left in October are potatoes and pumpkins.

The Stonewall Kitchen secret to enjoying an abundance of flavorful vegetables and side dishes all year long is to combine nature's seasonal offerings with our seasonless condiments. For instance, in winter, we pair roasted beets with a splash of Aged Balsamic Vinegar. In summer, we perk up fresh green beans with a touch of Roasted Garlic & Onion Jam. And we add flavor to our favorite mashed potatoes with Basil Pesto Mustard all year round.

Green Beans
with Gorgonzola

As the sun rises over the vegetable patches of Maine in mid-summer, gardeners can already be seen harvesting green beans. The scene replays itself for weeks, as the beans continue to grow throughout the rest of the season. (The vines may not climb up to the sky, but with the amount of beans they produce, they appear magical anyway.) Quickly blanching green beans helps maintain their bright color and crisp texture. Glazing them with a savory jam or chutney and sprinkling them with cheese takes them to a whole new level. If some of your guests don't like blue cheese, substitute another cheese such as feta or Boursin, or simply serve the crumbled blue cheese on the side for sprinkling.

2 pounds green beans

2 tablespoons extra virgin olive oil

3 tablespoons Roasted Garlic & Onion Jam or mango chutney

6 ounces blue cheese, such as Gorgonzola

¼ cup sliced, blanched almonds

Bring 2 quarts salted water to a boil in a large saucepan set over high heat. Add the beans and return the water to a boil. Boil until the beans are partially cooked but still snap when broken, about 3 minutes. Drain the beans in a colander set in the sink and run cold water over them until they are cold. Drain well.

Heat the oil in a large skillet over medium-high heat. Add the beans and cook for 3 minutes. Reduce the heat to low, add the jam, and cook, stirring constantly, until the jam is completely melted. Toss the beans as the jam melts to ensure that they are all well coated.

Transfer the beans to a large serving platter. Crumble the blue cheese over the top and sprinkle with the almonds. Serve immediately.

MAKES 6 TO 8 SERVINGS

Balsamic Roasted Beets

Nearly every Maine farmhouse has a root cellar, the winter storage place for beets, potatoes, carrots, and other sturdy root vegetables—our staples until spring thaws the ground, allowing the soft shoots of peas and asparagus to sprout again. These beets are one of our favorites—simply roasted and dressed with a pan sauce of a little warm balsamic vinegar. Spoon them over crisp, chilled greens, or cover and refrigerate them overnight, allowing them to absorb more of the sauce for a richer taste. Hot or cold, they can accompany any roasted meat.

Preheat the oven to 400°F.

Toss the beets with the oil, salt, and pepper in a large mixing bowl until well coated. Pour the beets into a roasting pan large enough to hold them in one layer without crowding.

Roast the beets for 25 minutes, shaking the pan occasionally, or until they are just tender when pierced with the tip of a sharp knife. Remove from the oven and immediately pour the vinegar into the hot pan. Stir with a wooden spoon to coat the beets well and to scrape up any juices that have caramelized on the bottom of the pan.

Serve the beets hot, at room temperature, or cold. They will keep for up to 3 days covered in the refrigerator.

1½ pounds beets, peeled and cut into ½-inch cubes

3 tablespoons extra virgin olive oil

1 teaspoon kosher salt

¼ teaspoon freshly ground black pepper

2 tablespoons Aged Balsamic Vinegar

MAKES 4 SERVINGS

Sweet and Salty Roasted Fennel

The faintly green bulbs of fennel, sometimes confused with anise, sport green celery-like stalks tipped with lacy and delicate, wispy fronds. The crunchy bulb, which has a mild licorice flavor, can be slivered and served raw in a salad, or, as in this recipe, roasted. It is a favorite in Italian cooking, so it's not surprising that our Sun-Dried Tomato and Olive Relish goes so well with it. If there are any leftovers, they'd make excellent vegetarian sandwiches.

Preheat the oven to 375°F.

Remove any tough outer layers and cut the fennel lengthwise into ½-inch slices, making sure that each slice contains a piece of the core (this will keep the fennel from falling apart as it roasts).

Pour the oil into a roasting pan large enough to hold the fennel slices in one layer. Place the fennel in the pan and turn to coat it in oil. Sprinkle with the salt. Bake the fennel for 10 minutes. Turn the slices over with a spatula and bake for another 10 minutes. Top each slice of fennel with 1 tablespoon of the relish and 1 tablespoon of the cheese (if using). Bake for 5 minutes more, or until the relish is warmed through and the cheese is begining to melt. Use a large spatula to remove the fennel from the pan, without dislodging the topping.

Serve immediately, or let the fennel cool and serve at room temperature. The fennel will keep for up to 24 hours covered in the refrigerator.

3 fennel bulbs, trimmed

¼ cup extra virgin olive oil

½ teaspoon salt

½ cup Sun-Dried Tomato and Olive Relish or chopped Marinated Sun-Dried Tomatoes

½ cup shredded Parmigiano-Reggiano, optional

MAKES 4 TO 6 SERVINGS

Oven-Roasted Spiced Fries

We frequently travel to the farmer's market in Portsmouth where we first sold our preserves. We visit with old friends and pick up local vegetables, such as Butte or Maine fingerling potatoes for this recipe. Both of these have an earthy flavor that we like, but they are small and less starchy, so we use them whole or sometimes cut them in half lengthwise. If you can't find them, any baking or waxy potatoes will do for this recipe, whichever potato you use, a spice rub creates a savory crust (no need to salt the fries). We like to serve these with any of our chutneys instead of ketchup.

Preheat the oven to 450°F.

Cut each potato crosswise in half, then cut each half into 6 wedges. Blot the potatoes dry with paper towels and place them in a large mixing bowl. Drizzle the oil over the potatoes and toss until they are well coated. Add the spice rub and toss until the spices are evenly distributed.

Transfer the potatoes to a roasting pan large enough to hold them in one layer. With a rubber spatula, scrape out any oil and spices that remain in the bowl onto the potatoes.

Roast the potatoes for about 45 minutes, turning them once or twice so they don't stick to the pan. They are done when they are evenly browned, crisp on the outside, and tender on the inside. Serve hot.

3 pounds baking potatoes (about 3 large potatoes), scrubbed

⅓ cup Roasted Garlic Oil or olive oil

1 tablespoon Spice Rub for Vegetables or your favorite spice mixture

MAKES 4 TO 6 SERVINGS

Pesto Mashed Potatoes

Potatoes like Katahdin or Kennebec are typically used for mashed potatoes, though Red Norland, with their deep red color, fluffy texture, and rich flavor are a real treat if you can find them. Whichever kind you choose, if you leave the skins on the potatoes, you preserve much of the vitamin content and give an appealingly rustic character to the dish. A generous amount of Basil Pesto Mustard from our pantry gives these potatoes their delicious flavor.

Cut the potatoes into quarters and place them in a large pot. Add enough water to cover the potatoes by 3 inches, bring to a boil over medium-high heat, and boil the potatoes until they are just tender when pierced with the tip of a sharp knife, about 20 minutes.

Drain the potatoes into a colander, put them back into the pot and add the milk over low heat. Mash the potatoes until they are nearly smooth using a potato masher or a hand-held electric mixer; leave a few lumps for texture.

Beat in the mustard, cheese, and oil using a large wooden spoon until the cheese melts and the mustard is thoroughly incorporated. Season with salt and pepper. Serve immediately.

2 pounds Katahdin or Kennebec potatoes

1 cup whole milk

¼ cup Basil Pesto Mustard or hearty mustard

½ cup shredded Parmigiano-Reggiano

2 tablespoons extra virgin olive oil

Salt and freshly ground black pepper to taste

MAKES 6 SERVINGS

Bombay Potato Salad

Bombay Potato Salad

Curry powder—mild or hot, whichever you prefer—gives this robust, chunky salad the flavor of India, and we spice it up even more with almonds, peas, and yogurt, and our Red Chili and Honey Mustard. Serve it instead of old-fashioned salad with fried chicken, cold roast beef sandwiches, or hamburgers and hot dogs.

3 pounds small red-skinned potatoes

1 cup frozen petite peas (do not use canned peas)

½ cup slivered almonds

½ cup plain yogurt

¼ cup Red Chili and Honey Mustard or Dijon mustard

2 tablespoons mayonnaise

1½ tablespoons curry powder (mild or hot)

⅓ cup chopped cilantro

2 teaspoons cider vinegar

Salt and freshly ground black pepper to taste

Place the potatoes in a large saucepan and add water to cover them by at least 2 inches. Place the pan over high heat and bring to a boil. Reduce the heat to medium and boil the potatoes until they are just tender when pierced with the tip of a knife, about 20 minutes. Drain in a colander.

Cut the potatoes in half or into quarters, depending on how chunky you like your potato salad. (If the potatoes are too hot to handle at this point, use a kitchen towel to protect your hand.) Place the potatoes in a large mixing bowl and scatter the peas over them (the heat from the potatoes will begin to defrost the peas). Set aside.

Place the almonds in a medium skillet and toast them over high heat, shaking the pan gently and tossing until they are lightly golden, about 3 minutes. (If they start to burn around the edges, lower the heat to medium.) Add the nuts to the peas and potatoes.

Combine the yogurt, mustard, mayonnaise, curry powder, cilantro, and vinegar in small bowl, stirring until well blended, and season with salt and pepper. Pour over the potatoes and gently toss them using a large rubber spatula, just until the vegetables are well coated. (Overmixing may mash the potatoes.) This salad is best the day after it's made, when the flavors have had a chance to blend and mellow. It will keep for up to 2 days in the refrigerator in a tightly covered container.

MAKES 8 SERVINGS

Swiss Chard with Bacon and Garlic

At the farmer's market you may find Swiss chard in a variety of colors: white, red, orange, and yellow. (Actually, only the stems and veins vary in color; the leaves are always green.) You can mix and match the different varieties for a colorful dish. Look for bunches with undamaged, dark green leaves that are firm and curled slightly at the edges. Chard is a sturdy green. We like to steam it, then toss it with bacon and toasted pecans and drizzle it with a little flavored oil just before serving.

1½ pounds Swiss chard, rinsed but not dried

⅓ cup pecan pieces

¼ pound bacon (4 to 5 slices), cut into 1-inch pieces

2 tablespoons Roasted Garlic Oil or olive oil

Cut the stems from the chard and slice the leaves crosswise into thirds. Set the chard aside.

Toast the pecans in a large skillet over medium-low heat until fragrant and lightly brown, about 3 minutes. Shake the pan often to prevent the nuts from burning. Transfer the nuts to a small bowl and set aside.

Add the bacon to the skillet and sauté over medium heat, stirring occasionally, until crisp, about 7 minutes. Transfer the bacon to another small bowl, using a slotted spoon. Pour out all but 2 teaspoons of the bacon fat from the skillet.

Place the pan back over medium heat for 30 seconds. Add the chard—be careful, as the water clinging to the leaves will splatter when it hits the hot fat. Turn the leaves over using two long wooden spoons and reduce the heat to low. Cover the skillet tightly (use aluminum foil if necessary) and allow the chard to steam for about 12 minutes, or until just tender.

At this point, there should be 2 to 3 tablespoons liquid in the bottom of the skillet. If there is too little liquid and the chard is sticking to the pan, add

2 to 3 tablespoons of water. If there is too much liquid, raise the heat to medium-high and boil until the liquid reduces to the proper amount. Turn off the heat and add the nuts and bacon. Toss quickly until well distributed. Drizzle with the oil and serve immediately.

MAKES 4 TO 6 SERVINGS

Three-Color Slaw

This crunchy salad goes with almost anything—from burgers to roast chicken. Jícama, which looks something like a squat potato, is a root vegetable with a thick, fibrous beige skin that must be removed before eating. Inside is crisp white flesh with a mildly sweet taste.

Shred the jícama, carrots, and cabbage in a food processor or with a grater. Place the vegetables in a large mixing bowl. Add the dressing and toss until the vegetables are evenly mixed and coated with dressing. Season with salt and pepper.

Serve chilled or at room temperature. The salad will keep for up to 3 days covered in the refrigerator.

1 medium jícama (about 1 pound), peeled

1 pound carrots, peeled

½ small red cabbage (about 1 pound), halved and cored

1 cup Dill Mustard Dressing or your favorite dressing

Salt and freshly ground black pepper to taste

MAKES 8 SERVINGS

Snow Peas and Water Chestnuts

Our Roasted Red Pepper Vinaigrette gives a new dimension to this Asian-style vegetable dish. Serve it alongside roast meats or use it to make even the simplest grilled dinner, like barbecued chicken or hamburgers, special. Water chestnuts and sesame oil are available in most supermarkets in the Asian foods section.

Place the snow peas in a medium skillet and add 2 cups water. Place the skillet over medium heat and bring to a simmer. Cover the pan and blanch the snow peas for 2 to 3 minutes. Drain the snow peas in a colander.

Add the vinaigrette, soy sauce, sesame oil, and ginger to the skillet over medium heat. Stir until everything is well combined and the sauce comes to a simmer. Add the water chestnuts and snow peas and simmer for 30 seconds, or until the vegetables are heated through. Transfer the vegetables and sauce to a serving bowl and sprinkle with the sesame seeds. Serve immediately.

½ pound snow peas

⅓ cup Roasted Red Pepper Vinaigrette or pureed jarred pimientos

2 teaspoons soy sauce

2 teaspoons toasted sesame oil

½ teaspoon finely grated ginger

One 8-ounce can sliced water chestnuts, drained and rinsed

1 teaspoon sesame seeds

MAKES 4 SERVINGS

Desserts

We can't think of a faster way to add concentrated fruit flavor to cakes, cookies, or ice cream than with preserves from our pantry. Sweet and rich, jam has a dessert-like quality right out of the jar. We even created our Wild Maine Blueberry Jam to taste just like one of our favorite desserts: the blueberry pie Jim's grandmother, Hannah, used to make.

We use Strawberry Apple Rhubarb Jam to complement the flavor of the fresh fruit in our recipe for Baked Bananas. We sweeten Apple Cheddar Crisp with Orange Cranberry Marmalade—it marries well with the flavor of the apples but is strong enough to balance the rich cheese topping. We also spoon a wide variety of our favorite jams, jellies, and marmalades onto our Thumbprint Cookies.

The natural fruit sugars in Stonewall Kitchen jams concentrate as they are cooked. That's why our dessert recipes often call for less sugar than others. In fact, some of our recipes don't require any added sugar at all. It's another example of how contemporary pantry cooking can add more flavor with fewer ingredients and in less time.

Blueberry Ice Cream

Blueberry fields (known as barrens) cover rocky hills all over eastern Maine. Maine blueberries are unique—tiny, dark beads, often no more than a quarter inch in diameter, with an intense flavor that belies their size, grown no more than a foot off the ground. We've captured that flavor in our Wild Maine Blueberry Jam—and in this ice cream, a quintessential Stonewall Kitchen dessert.

Combine the cream and half-and-half in a medium saucepan and heat over medium heat just until small bubbles appear around the edges of the cream. Do not boil. Immediately remove the pan from the heat and add the jam. Stir until the jam is completely melted and incorporated. Pour the mixture into a medium bowl or a pitcher, cover, and place in the refrigerator until cold, at least 6 hours.

Stir the blueberry syrup and vanilla into the cold ice cream mixture. Freeze in an ice cream machine according to the manufacturer's instructions. When it's finished, the ice cream will be soft but ready to eat. For firmer ice cream, transfer the ice cream to an airtight freezer container and place in the freezer for at least 4 hours. Serve the ice cream with fresh berries and whipped cream on top. The ice cream will keep for up to 1 week.

1 cup heavy cream

1 cup half-and-half

One 13-ounce jar Wild Maine Blueberry Jam or blueberry preserves

2 tablespoons blueberry syrup

2 teaspoons vanilla extract

1 cup blueberries (about ½ pint)

1 cup heavy cream, whipped

MAKES 1 QUART

Coconut Peach Sorbet

Coconut Peach Sorbet

Our Republic of Tea jams are perfect for cooking. With both fruit and herbal flavors, they allow you to add layers of flavor to a dessert with just one ingredient. In this recipe, Ginger Peach Tea Jam is blended with coconut milk for a sorbet that has a traditional Southeast Asian taste. Don't confuse rich, creamy unsweetened coconut milk with sweetened cream of coconut (used to make piña coladas). The sorbet is sublime when made with just these two ingredients, but we sometimes add a chopped, ripe peach and crystallized ginger to underline its complex flavors.

One 13-ounce jar Ginger Peach Tea Jam or peach jam

One 14-ounce can unsweetened coconut milk

1 small peach, pitted and roughly chopped, optional

2 teaspoons chopped crystallized ginger, optional

Combine the jam and coconut milk in a blender and blend thoroughly on high. Add the peach and ginger (if using), and pulse on and off two or three times to incorporate them without pureeing them. (A few small pieces will add texture to the sorbet.) Place the blender container in the refrigerator until the mixture is cold, about 2 hours.

Pour the mixture into an ice cream maker and freeze according to the manufacturer's instructions. When it's finished, the sorbet will be soft but ready to eat. Transfer the sorbet to an airtight freezer container and place it in the freezer to firm up if desired—this can take from 4 hours to overnight, depending on your freezer.

Serve the sorbet with sliced fresh peaches and gingersnaps. Store the sorbet covered in the freezer for up to 1 week.

MAKES ABOUT 1 QUART

Blueberry Sour Cream
Coffee Cake

You can always tell when we're baking this Bundt cake in our stores—the air fills with the perfume of blueberries and customers linger, waiting for a taste. Our Wild Maine Blueberry Jam creates a ribbon of blueberry filling in the middle of the cake. Although we serve it for dessert, it is also great for breakfast or brunch or a midafternoon snack. Sometimes we add a splash of rum to the melted jam that is drizzled over the top of the cake.

Preheat the oven to 350°F. Butter and flour a 10-inch Bundt pan.

Sift together the flour, baking powder, and salt in a medium bowl. Set aside.

Using an electric mixer on high, beat the butter in a large mixing bowl until soft and creamy. Add the sugar and beat until fluffy. Beat in the eggs, one at a time, making sure the first egg is well incorporated before adding the second. Add the sour cream and vanilla and beat until the mixture is smooth. Turn the mixer to low, add the flour mixture, and beat just until incorporated.

Transfer ½ cup of the batter to a small mixing bowl and set aside. Pour the remaining batter into the prepared pan and smooth the top. Make a 1-inch trough in the center of the batter all the way around the pan. Add ¾ cup of the blueberry jam into the served batter and beat with the electric mixer until thoroughly combined. Spoon the blueberry batter evenly into the trough.

Bake for 1 hour, or until the cake begins to pull away from the edges of the pan and a skewer inserted in the center of the cake comes out clean. Cool the cake in the pan for 15 minutes, then invert the cake onto a wire rack. Cool the cake completely on the rack.

- 2 cups all-purpose flour, plus additional for the pan
- 1 tablespoon baking powder
- ½ teaspoon salt
- ½ pound (2 sticks) unsalted butter, at room temperature, plus additional for the pan
- 1½ cups granulated sugar
- 2 large eggs, at room temperature
- 1 cup sour cream
- 1 teaspoon vanilla extract
- ¾ cup plus 1 tablespoon Wild Maine Blueberry Jam or blueberry preserves
- 2 tablespoons gold rum, optional
- 1 tablespoon confectioners' sugar

Melt the remaining 1 tablespoon blueberry jam in a small pan over low heat. (Alternatively, melt the jam in a small bowl in the microwave on medium for 15 seconds.) Stir the rum (if using) into the melted jam. Sift the confectioners' sugar over the cake and drizzle with the melted jam. Serve immediately, or store the cake in an airtight container at room temperature for up to 3 days. The cake can also be frozen for up to 1 month. Defrost at room temperature before serving.

MAKES ONE 10-INCH BUNDT CAKE

Baked Bananas

This Maine version of Bananas Foster, the famous New Orleans specialty of bananas sautéed in butter with brown sugar and rum, adds Strawberry Apple Rhubarb Jam to the rich sauce. The aroma of bananas fills the kitchen as the dessert bakes, and it's hard to wait for the dish to cool for a few minutes before topping it with vanilla ice cream and digging in.

Preheat the oven to 450°F. Butter a 14-inch oval or 8 × 11-inch rectangular baking dish.

Slice the bananas into ½-inch rounds. Arrange the banana slices in the baking dish, overlapping them as necessary. Pour the rum over the bananas. Drop teaspoonfuls of the jam evenly over the bananas. Sprinkle the vanilla and cinnamon over the top and dot evenly with the butter.

Cover the baking dish tightly with aluminum foil and bake for 20 minutes, or until the bananas are soft and the jam, butter, and rum have melted together, creating a bubbling, syrupy sauce. Allow the bananas to cool for 5 minutes.

Spoon the bananas into dessert bowls and top each with a scoop of vanilla ice cream. Drizzle some of the sauce over the ice cream and serve immediately.

4 large bananas, peeled

¼ cup gold rum

½ cup Strawberry Apple Rhubarb Jam or strawberry jam

2 teaspoons vanilla extract

½ teaspoon ground cinnamon

2 tablespoons unsalted butter, at room temperature, plus additional for the baking dish

1 pint vanilla ice cream

MAKES 4 TO 6 SERVINGS

Thumbprint Cookies

These cookies are traditionally made by adding the jam to the cookies before baking them, but that can dull the look and taste of the preserves. Since we're rather partial to jam, we prefer to add it just after the cookies come out of the oven—it melts into the hollows of the warm cookies where it glistens like jewels, and its flavor is much brighter. Make these cookies with one favorite preserve, or take the opportunity to use up any odds and ends of jams and jellies you may have in the refrigerator.

Preheat the oven to 375°F.

Cream the butter and sugar in a large bowl with an electric mixer set on medium. Add the egg yolks and vanilla and beat until the mixture is smooth and creamy. Turn the mixer to low, add the salt and flour, and mix until a soft dough forms.

Lightly beat the egg white in a small bowl. Roll the dough into 1-inch balls between your palms. Dip the balls one at a time into the beaten egg white and then roll each one in the chopped nuts until completely covered.

Place the balls 1 inch apart on an ungreased cookie sheet and bake for 5 minutes. Use 2 cookie sheets and bake the cookies in batches, if necessary.

Remove the sheet from the oven and use your thumb or the end of a wooden spoon handle to create a deep indentation in the middle of each cookie. The cookies will crack around the edges and flatten out a bit when you press into them—this is okay.

½ pound (2 sticks) unsalted butter, at room temperature

½ cup packed light brown sugar

2 large egg yolks

2 teaspoons vanilla extract

½ teaspoon salt

2 cups all-purpose flour

1 large egg white

1¼ cups finely ground walnuts

½ cup jam, jelly, or marmalade (see headnote)

Place the cookie sheet back in the oven and bake for an additional 10 minutes, or until the cookies are just beginning to turn brown around the edges and are brown on the bottom. Remove the cookie sheet from the oven and immediately fill the indentation in each cookie with a generous ½ teaspoon of the jam. Transfer the cookies to a rack to cool.

Store the cookies in one layer in an airtight container at room temperature. They will keep for up to 1 week.

**MAKES ABOUT
30 COOKIES**

Honey Nut Oatmeal Bars

These bars are light and crisp, rather than chewy—something like a granola bar, but a little less sweet. Using a jar of our Mixed Nuts in Clover Honey means fewer ingredients to measure out—and heaps of flavor.

Preheat the oven to 350°F. Generously grease a 9 × 13-inch Pyrex baking dish.

Place the jar of nuts and honey in a bowl of very hot water and set aside until the honey has softened and the mixture can be stirred easily.

Place the oats, flour, cinnamon, and salt in a medium bowl and mix until well combined.

Cream the butter and brown sugar in a large bowl with an electric mixer set on medium. Add the peanut butter and beat until smooth. Stir in the nuts and honey, along with the vanilla and coconut. Add the dry ingredients and mix until everything is well combined. The texture will be more like that of a firm cookie dough than a batter. Use your hands if necessary to complete the mixing.

Press the dough evenly into the prepared pan, using your hands. Make sure the dough reaches to all the corners.

Bake for 30 minutes, or until lightly brown around the edges. Remove the pan from the oven and immediately run a small sharp knife around the edges of the pan to loosen the bars. Cover the pan with a cookie sheet or cutting board and turn upside down to release the bars. If desired, gently place a second cutting board or cookie sheet on top of the bars and invert again so the bars are right side up. Allow to cool completely, then cut into bars using a long sharp knife. Store the bars in an airtight container at room temperature for up to 1 week.

One 12¼-ounce jar Mixed Nuts in Clover Honey

1½ cups quick-cooking rolled oats (not instant)

1 cup all-purpose flour

1 teaspoon ground cinnamon

¼ teaspoon salt

8 tablespoons (1 stick) unsalted butter, at room temperature. plus additional for the baking dish

½ cup packed light brown sugar

¼ cup creamy peanut butter

1 teaspoon vanilla extract

½ cup packed sweetened shredded coconut

MAKES 16 BARS

Peach Melba Shortcakes

This recipe is a new twist on an old favorite. Instead of the traditional strawberries, we fill these shortcakes with peaches, our Raspberry Peach Champagne Jam and, of course, whipped cream. The key to the dessert's success is in choosing ripe peaches. Just remember: If it smells like a peach, it will taste like a peach. There's no better accompaniment to this shortcake than a flute of Champagne.

TO PREPARE THE SHORTCAKES

Position a rack in the center of the oven and preheat the oven to 400°F.

Sift together the flour, 3 tablespoons of the granulated sugar, the baking soda, and salt into a large mixing bowl. Cut the butter into the dry ingredients using a pastry cutter or two knives until the mixture resembles small peas. Add the cream and stir with a wooden spoon just until a soft dough forms.

Turn the dough out onto a floured surface and pat it out with the palms of your hands until it is ¾ inch thick. Cut out 4-inch circles using a round cookie cutter or an inverted glass. Press the dough scraps together if necessary, pat out, and cut out more circles: You need a total of 6 circles. Brush the tops of the circles with the milk, using a pastry brush, and sprinkle with the remaining 2 teaspoons of sugar.

Place the circles 2 inches apart on an ungreased cookie sheet. Bake for 15 minutes, or until the shortcakes are lightly brown and sound hollow when tapped. Remove the sheet from the oven and cool the shortcakes on a rack. The shortcakes can be made up to 1 day ahead and stored in an airtight container at room temperature.

For the shortcakes

2 cups all-purpose flour

3 tablespoons plus 2 teaspoons granulated sugar

1 tablespoon baking soda

½ teaspoon salt

8 tablespoons (1 stick) unsalted butter, at room temperature

¾ cup light cream

¼ cup whole milk

TO PREPARE THE FILLING

Combine the cream, confectioners' sugar, and vanilla in a medium bowl and whip, using a whisk or an electric mixer set on medium, until the cream just holds soft peaks.

Combine the jam and liqueur in a small bowl and stir until well blended.

TO ASSEMBLE THE DISH

Split the shortcakes horizontally. Spread 1½ tablespoons of the jam over the cut side of each bottom and top with 6 peach slices and a large dollop of whipped cream. Cover with the shortcake lids and garnish with any remaining whipped cream.

Serve immediately.

For the filling

1 cup heavy cream

1 tablespoon confectioners' sugar

1 teaspoon vanilla extract

½ cup Raspberry Peach Champagne Jam or raspberry jam

2 tablespoons raspberry liqueur or raspberry syrup

6 large peaches, peeled, pitted, and sliced into eighths

MAKES 6 SERVINGS

Apple-Cheddar Crisp

With this recipe, Chef Stephanie Duryea of Walter's Café in Portland, Maine, turned one of our favorite desserts—apple pie topped with cheese—into a comforting crisp using our Orange Cranberry Marmalade. Pick firm baking apples, such as Cortland or Rome, so the slices hold their shape in the oven.

Preheat the oven to 350°F. Generously butter a 9 × 13-inch baking pan.

TO PREPARE THE FILLING

Peel, halve, and core the apples. Cut them into ½-inch pieces and place them in a large bowl. Pour the lemon juice over them, tossing to coat them completely. Add the marmalade, sugar, salt, and nutmeg and mix until the apples and marmalade are well combined.

TO PREPARE THE TOPPING

Combine the flour, oats, brown sugar, and cinnamon in a large bowl, mixing well. Add the butter and cut it into the flour mixture using a pastry cutter or two knives, until the mixture resembles coarse meal; no pieces of butter should be visible.

TO ASSEMBLE THE DISH

Pour the apple mixture into the prepared pan. Sprinkle the topping evenly over the apples. Bake for 45 minutes, or until the apples are bubbling and the topping has just begun to brown. Remove the pan from the oven and sprinkle the cheese evenly over the top of the hot crisp; the heat of the crisp will melt the cheese. If desired, place the crisp under the broiler for 30 seconds, or until the cheese begins to bubble and turn brown.

Allow the crisp to cool for at least 10 minutes before serving. Serve hot or warm.

For the filling

7 large baking apples

2 tablespoons fresh lemon juice, strained

One 13-ounce jar Orange Cranberry Marmalade or orange marmalade

½ cup sugar

1 teaspoon salt

½ teaspoon grated nutmeg

For the topping

½ cup all-purpose flour

1 cup quick-cooking rolled oats (not instant)

1 cup packed light brown sugar

1 teaspoon ground cinnamon

½ pound (2 sticks) cold unsalted butter, cut into small pieces, plus additional for the baking pan

1½ cups shredded sharp Cheddar (about 6 ounces)

MAKES 6 TO 8 SERVINGS

Strawberries in Orange-Balsamic Vinegar Sauce

If you've ever tasted ripe strawberries plucked from the vine—plump, sweet, and still warm from the sun—you might wonder why we'd want to add anything to this luscious fruit. But aged balsamic vinegar, mildly sweet and syrupy, highlights the flavor of the berries. And a touch of Grand Marnier elevates them to another level. Serve them on their own, or with a scoop of orange sorbet or a dollop of crème fraîche.

Combine the strawberries, sugar, and orange zest in a medium bowl, tossing until the berries are well coated with sugar. Set aside to macerate for 15 minutes.

Add the Grand Marnier and vinegar. Toss gently until well combined. Serve immediately.

1 quart strawberries, hulled and sliced into thirds

2 tablespoons sugar

1½ tablespoons grated orange zest

¼ cup Grand Marnier or Blood Orange Syrup

¼ cup Aged Balsamic Vinegar

MAKES 6 SERVINGS

Drinks

Drinks before dinner? We like to keep it simple. And local. In Maine, small vintners produce apéritif wines made from local blueberries, rhubarb, or pears. And many a coastal town now has its own microbrewery, producing beer and ale that have become as synonymous with the area as lobster and L. L. Bean. We keep plenty of these local specialties on hand for unexpected company.

But we never forget the basics—martinis, margaritas, and cosmopolitans. Our recipes for these classics all have a twist. Not a lemon or lime twist, but a splash of something from our pantry, Blood Orange or Raspberry Syrup. We can't offer cocktails in our stores, but if you stop by in the middle of summer, you might find us serving a large pitcher of Strawberry Lemonade. In winter, there's always a warm pot of cider mixed with a few spices and a little Apple Butter Syrup.

With these easy recipes, you can relax and enjoy the taste of Maine wherever you live.

Strawberry Lemonade

From the beaches in York to the mountains in Acadia National Park, Maine offers thousands of quiet nooks with gorgeous vistas, perfect for laying down a blanket and enjoying a Stonewall picnic. Whatever else is on the menu, we always bring along a large thermos of this tart-sweet pink lemonade. The color comes from the red berries, and although fresh fruit is our preference, frozen berries will work fine. (Frozen strawberries collapse and lose their shape when they defrost, so measure them while they're frozen, then let them defrost.)

Combine the lemon juice and sugar in a 3-quart pitcher and stir until the sugar is completely dissolved.

Set aside 2 large berries for garnish and place the rest of the berries in a blender. Add the corn syrup and 2 tablespoons water and blend until the berries are pureed.

Pour the berry puree into the pitcher with the lemon juice mixture, add 4 ½ cups cold water, and stir until well combined. The lemonade can be made up to 24 hours in advance. Keep covered in the refrigerator.

Thinly slice the reserved strawberries, and add the strawberries and lemon slices to the pitcher. Add ice to fill the pitcher and stir until the lemonade is cold. Serve over ice in tall glasses.

1 cup fresh lemon juice, strained

1 cup sugar

4 cups strawberries, hulled

2 tablespoons light corn syrup

1 lemon, thinly sliced

MAKES ABOUT 2 QUARTS

Blood Orange Martini

The waters off the Maine coast are dotted with tiny islands reachable only by ferry. They offer privacy, and often more important, they offer ocean sunsets over the Atlantic. We like to toast the ocean view with a martini the same color as a glorious Maine sunset, made with an ounce or two of bright red Blood Orange Syrup. Blood oranges, a Mediterranean native, are increasingly available here during their winter season. Their rind may have only the slightest hint of red, but the fruit inside can be solid crimson.

3 ounces gin

2 ounces Blood Orange Syrup or orange syrup

½ ounce white vermouth

Two 4-inch-long strips orange zest (removed with a vegetable peeler)

Fill two martini glasses with ice. Fill with water and set the glasses aside to chill while you prepare the drinks.

Fill a cocktail shaker three-quarters full with ice. Add the gin, syrup, and vermouth. Stir with a long spoon for 20 seconds, or until the outside of the shaker is frosted.

Empty the martini glasses. Strain the martini mixture into them. Garnish each glass with a strip of orange zest and serve immediately.

MAKES 2 SERVINGS

Stonewall Margarita

The classic margarita combines tequila, lime juice, and orange liqueur. Most bars use bottled lime juice, but we prefer fresh. We balance the acidity of the juice with our sweet Blood Orange Syrup. As for tequila, we recommend a 100 percent blue agave, high-quality brand for the best taste. (And, living on the ocean, we wouldn't coat the rim of our margarita glasses with anything but sea salt.) Serve these margaritas "up" (without ice) in stemmed 6-ounce cocktail or martini glasses.

1 cup fine sea salt

2 limes, halved

4 ounces tequila

3 ounces Blood Orange Syrup or orange syrup

Pour the salt onto a flat plate slightly larger than the diameter of your cocktail glasses. Rub the cut side of 1 cut lime half around the rim of each glass to wet the edges. Turn the glasses upside down and dip them into the salt to coat the rims.

Fill a cocktail shaker three-quarters full with ice. Add the tequila and blood orange syrup. Squeeze the juice from the lime halves into the shaker. Cover and shake vigorously until frost appears on the outside of the shaker, about 20 seconds.

Carefully strain the drinks into the prepared glasses and serve immediately.

MAKES 2 SERVINGS

Hot Apple-Buttered Rum

Maine has long, cold winters. The trees turn in September, the mill ponds freeze by November, and then our tulips don't bloom until the thaw in late May. We don't get much snow by the coast, but a bone-chilling fog can set in and linger for months on end. Sometimes hot spiced cider, enriched with Stonewall Kitchen Apple Butter Syrup and a little rum, is just the thing to take the nip out of the season.

Combine the cider, syrup, cloves, and cinnamon in a small saucepan. Bring to a simmer over low heat and allow the mixture to simmer for 5 minutes.

Pour 1½ ounces rum into each of two mugs. Add the cider mixture, making sure the spices are evenly distributed between the mugs. Sprinkle each mug with a small pinch of nutmeg and serve immediately.

2 cups apple cider

3 ounces Apple Butter Syrup or Maine Maple Syrup

4 whole cloves

2 cinnamon sticks

3 ounces gold rum or brandy

Pinch of grated nutmeg

MAKES 2 SERVINGS

Raspberry Cosmopolitan

Add cranberry juice to vodka and you have a Cape Codder. Add a splash of orange liqueur and a squeeze of lime, and you're sipping the trendy Cosmopolitan. Substitute Stonewall Kitchen Raspberry Syrup for the cranberry juice and the drink becomes our own Maine-style cocktail.

Fill a cocktail shaker three-quarters full with ice. Add the vodka, Cointreau, raspberry syrup, and lime juice. Cover and shake vigorously until frost appears on the outside of the shaker, about 20 seconds.

Strain the drinks into two 8-ounce cocktail glasses filled with ice. Garnish with the raspberries and serve immediately.

4 ounces vodka

2 ounces Cointreau or other orange liqueur

2 ounces Raspberry Syrup

Juice of 2 limes

6 raspberries

MAKES 2 SERVINGS

Stonewall Kitchen Products

Jams, Jellies & Marmalades

Orange Cranberry Marmalade
Lemon Pear Marmalade
Raspberry Peach Champagne Jam
Strawberry & Brandied Apricot Jam
Wild Maine Blueberry Jam
Roasted Garlic & Onion Jam
Strawberry Apple Rhubarb Jam
Red Pepper Jelly
Apricot Cherry Jam
Cherry Chipotle Jam
Pineapple Mint Jam
Pink Grapefruit Marmalade
Sugar Plum Jam
Tomato Ginger Jam
Ginger Peach Tea Jam
Blackberry Sage Tea Jam
Raspberry Quince Tea Jam
Cinnamon Plum Tea Jam

Preserves

Boysenberry Preserve
Gooseberry Preserve
Lingonberry Preserve

Chutneys, Relishes & Sundries

Apple Cranberry Chutney
Old Farmhouse Chutney
Sun-Dried Tomato & Olive Relish
Artichoke & Caper Relish
Fresh Fennel Relish

Pasta Sauces

Amatriciana Marinara Sauce
Classic Marinara Sauce
Fire Roasted Pepper Marinara
 Sauce
Traditional Fresca Sauce
Sweet Onion & Pepper Fresca
 Sauce
Rosemary Balsamic Vinegar Fresca
 Sauce

Sauces

Lemon Dill Cocktail Sauce
Cranberry Horseradish Sauce
Maple Chipotle Grille Sauce
Roasted Garlic Peanut Sauce
Roasted Pepper Sesame Sauce
Vidalia Onion Fig Sauce
Curried Mango Grille Sauce

Mustards

Roasted Garlic Mustard
Basil Pesto Mustard
Onion & Jalapeño Mustard
Horseradish Mustard
Sun-Dried Tomato Mustard
Maine Maple Champagne Mustard
Bourbon Molassas Mustard
Curried Apricot Mustard
Lemon Peppercorn Mustard
Red Chili & Honey Mustard
Sesame Ginger Mustard

Dessert Toppings

Fresh Lemon Curd
Raspberry Liqueur Hot Fudge
Coffee Caramel Sauce
Fig & Walnut Butter
Mixed Nuts in Clover Honey

Syrups

Maine Maple Syrup
Wild Maine Blueberry Syrup
Apple Butter Syrup
Raspberry Syrup
Blood Orange Syrup

Pancake & Waffle Mix

Farmhouse Pancake & Waffle Mix

Vinaigrettes & Dressings

Roasted Garlic Vinaigrette
Roasted Red Pepper Vinaigrette
Lemon Peppercorn Vinaigrette
Dill Mustard Dressing—Fat Free
Maple Passion Dressing—Fat Free

Olive Oil & Balsamic Vinegar

Aged Balsamic Vinegar—Imported
from Italy
Extra Virgin Olive Oil—Imported
from Spain

Flavored Oils

Smoky Chipotle Chili Oil
Lemongrass Ginger Oil
Sun-Dried Tomato Basil Oil
Roasted Garlic Oil

Spice Rubs

Spice Rub for Chicken & Pork
Spice Rub for Seafood
Spice Rub for Steak & BBQ
Spice Rub for Vegetables

Canned Seafood Chowders & Bisques

New England Clam Chowder
New England Crab Bisque
New England Lobster Bisque

Downeast Crackers

Asiago Cheese Crackers
Cracked Black Peppercorn Crackers
Garden Herb Crackers
Roasted Garlic Crackers
Rosemary Parmesan Crackers
Simple White Crackers
Cheddar Dill Crackers

Stonewall Kitchen
Store Guide

Stonewall Lane
York, ME 03909
(207) 351-2712

13 Elm Street
Camden, ME 04843
(207) 236-8979

The Mall at Chestnut Hill
199 Boylston Street
Chestnut Hill, MA 02167
(617) 323-5258

182 Middle Street
Portland, ME 04101
(207) 679-2409

10 Pleasant Street
Portsmouth, NH 03802
(603) 422-7303

General home office telephone: *(207) 351-2713*

Ordering Number: *1 (800) 207-JAMS*

Fax: *(207) 351-2715*

Website: *www.stonewallkitchen.com*

Index

angel hair with walnut pesto, 63

appetizers, 45–59

    cocktail shrimp with roasted garlic mayonnaise, 50

    mango-Brie quesadillas, 48–49

    roasted garlic mayonnaise, 51

    savory herbed nuts, 52

    shrimp and chicken satay with two dipping
        sauces, 47

    spiced scones with smoked ham and Cherry
        Chipotle Jam, 59

    spicy white bean dip, 53

    sun-dried tomato salsa, 56

    sweet and savory crostini, 57

apple(s):

    baked, 8–9

    -buttered rum, hot, 153

    -Cheddar crisp, 143

    endive, and walnut salad, 71

bacon:

    -Cheddar sandwiches, gooey grilled, 34

    Swiss chard with garlic and, 124–25

baguette, smoked turkey with Roasted Garlic &
    Onion Jam on, 42

baked apples, 8–9

baked bananas, 135

baked beans, 112–13

baked macaroni and cheese, 65

balsamic roasted beets, 117

balsamic vinegar–orange sauce, strawberries in,
    147

bananas, baked, 135

bars, oatmeal honey nut, 139

basmati-orzo pilaf, toasted, swordfish kebabs with,
    85

bass, red pepper-sesame, 90–91

bean(s):

    baked, 112–13

    green, with Gorgonzola, 116

    white, spicy dip, 53

beef:

    flank steak fajitas, 105–6

    roast, with Old Farmhouse Chutney on rye, 43

beets, balsamic roasted, 117

beverages, *see* drinks

Blackberry Sage roast chicken, 101–2

black bread, egg salad on, 41

blood orange martini, 151

blueberry:
    ice cream, 130
    –maple granola, 7
    sour cream coffee cake, 133–34
Bombay potato salad, 123
breads:
    farmhouse buttermilk corn, 113
    French toast with cream cheese and jam filling,
      24
    jam muffins, 23
    jelly doughnuts, 25–26
    pumpkin-cranberry spice, 15
    spiced scones with smoked ham and Cherry
      Chipotle Jam, 59
    sweet and savory crostini, 57
    see also sandwiches
breakfast, 5–26
    baked apples, 8–9
    buttermilk pancakes, 19
    French toast with cream cheese and jam filling,
      24
    fried eggs with curry-browned butter and
      chutney, 13
    jam muffins, 23
    jelly doughnuts, 25–26
    jelly omelet, 17
    lobster eggs Benedict, 10, 12
    maple-blueberry granola, 7
    pumpkin-cranberry spice bread,
      15
    spicy Maine home fries, 14
Brie-mango quesadillas, 48–49
butter, curry-browned, fried eggs with chutney and,
    13
buttered rum, hot apple-, 153
buttermilk:
    farmhouse corn bread, 113
    pancakes, 19

cake, coffee, blueberry sour cream, 133–34
Cheddar:
    -apple crisp, 143
    -bacon sandwiches, gooey grilled, 34
cheese:
    apple-Cheddar crisp, 143
    baked macaroni and, 65
    cream, and jam filling, French toast with, 24
    gooey grilled Cheddar-bacon sandwiches, 34
    green beans with Gorgonzola, 116
    mango-Brie quesadillas, 48–49
    roasted eggplant and smoked mozzarella
      sandwiches, 38
Cherry Chipotle Jam, spiced scones with smoked
    ham and, 59
cherry walnut topping, 57
chicken:
    Blackberry Sage roast, 101–2
    Lemon Pear grilled, 99
    and shrimp satay with two dipping sauces,
      47
    stir-fried Tomato Ginger, 103
chowder, corn-crab, 31
chutney:
    fried eggs with curry-browned butter and, 13
    Old Farmhouse, roast beef on rye with, 43
cocktail shrimp with roasted garlic mayonnaise,
    50
coconut peach sorbet, 131
coffee cake, blueberry sour cream, 133–34
coleslaw, three-color, 126
cookies:
    honey nut oatmeal bars, 139
    thumbprint, 137–38
corn:
    bread, farmhouse buttermilk, 113
    -crab chowder, 31
cosmopolitan, raspberry, 154

crab:
  cakes, 92
  -corn chowder, 31
cranberry:
  horseradish vinaigrette, smoked trout salad with,
    69
  -pumpkin spice bread, 15
cream cheese and jam filling, French toast with,
  24
crisp, apple-Cheddar, 143
crostini, sweet and savory, 57
curry(ied):
  -browned butter and chutney, fried eggs with,
    13
  mango mayonnaise, 93
  prosciutto topping, 57

desserts, 129–47
  apple-Cheddar crisp, 143
  baked bananas, 135
  blueberry ice cream, 130
  blueberry sour cream coffee cake, 133–34
  coconut peach sorbet, 131
  honey nut oatmeal bars, 139
  peach Melba shortcakes, 141–42
  strawberries in orange–balsamic vinegar sauce,
    147
  thumbprint cookies, 137–38
dinner, Sunday ham, 112–13
dip, spicy white bean, 53
dipping sauces, two, shrimp and chicken satay with,
  47
doughnuts, jelly, 25–26
drinks, 149–54
  blood orange martini, 151
  hot apple-buttered rum, 153
  raspberry cosmopolitan, 154
  Stonewall margarita, 152
  strawberry lemonade, 150

egg(s):
  fried, with curry-browned butter and chutney,
    13
  jelly omelet, 17
  lobster Benedict, 10, 12
  salad on black bread, 41
eggplant, roasted, and smoked mozzarella
    sandwiches, 38
endive, apple, and walnut salad, 71

fajitas, flank steak, 105–6
farmhouse buttermilk corn bread, 113
fennel:
  penne with lemon, pine nuts and, 68
  sweet and salty roasted, 118
fish, see specific fish and seafood
flank steak fajitas, 105–6
French toast with cream cheese and jam filling,
    24
fried eggs with curry-browned butter and chutney,
    13
fries:
  home, spicy Maine, 14
  oven-roasted spiced, 119

garlic:
  roasted, mayonnaise, 51
  Swiss chard with bacon and, 124–25
gazpacho, year-round, 33
gooey grilled Cheddar-bacon sandwiches, 34
Gorgonzola, green beans with, 116
granola, maple-blueberry, 7
green beans with Gorgonzola, 116
grilled foods:
  gooey Cheddar-bacon sandwiches, 34
  Lemon Pear chicken, 99
  shrimp and chicken satay with two dipping
    sauces, 47
  spareribs with Vidalia Onion Fig Sauce, 107

ham:
  smoked, spiced scones with Cherry Chipotle Jam
    and, 59
  Sunday dinner, 112–13
herbed nuts, savory, 52
herb-mustard crust, rack of lamb with, 110
home fries, spicy Maine, 14
honey nut oatmeal bars, 139
horseradish cranberry vinaigrette, smoked trout salad
    with, 69
hot apple-buttered rum, 153

ice cream, blueberry, 130

jam:
  Cherry Chipotle, spiced scones with smoked ham
    and, 59
  and cream cheese filling, French toast with, 24
  Lingonberry, sesame-seared salmon with, 81
  muffins, 23
  Roasted Garlic & Onion, smoked turkey on
    baguette with, 42
jelly:
  doughnuts, 25–26
  omelet, 17

kebabs, swordfish, with toasted basmati-orzo pilaf, 85

lamb, rack of, with mustard-herb crust, 110
lemon, penne with fennel, pine nuts and, 68
lemonade, strawberry, 150
Lemon Pear grilled chicken, 99
Lingonberry Jam, sesame-seared salmon with, 81
linguine, spicy, with shrimp, 64
lobster:
  eggs Benedict, 10, 12
  roasted, 79
  rolls, Stonewall, 35
  tabbouleh salad, 75

macaroni and cheese, baked, 65
mango:
  -Brie quesadillas, 48–49
  curried mayonnaise, 93
  -peach soup, 32
maple-blueberry granola, 7
margarita, Stonewall, 152
martini, blood orange, 151
mashed potatoes, pesto, 122
mayonnaise:
  curried mango, 93
  roasted garlic, 51
meat, 97–113
  Blackberry Sage roast chicken, 101–2
  flank steak fajitas, 105–6
  Lemon Pear grilled chicken, 99
  Moroccan pork tenderloins, 111
  rack of lamb with mustard-herb crust, 110
  roast beef with Old Farmhouse Chutney on rye, 43
  spareribs with Vidalia Onion Fig Sauce, 107
  stir-fried Tomato Ginger chicken, 103
  Sunday ham dinner, 112–13
Moroccan pork tenderloins, 111
mozzarella, smoked, and roasted eggplant
    sandwiches, 38
muffins, jam, 23
mussels, steamed, 95
mustard-herb crust, rack of lamb with, 110

niçoise, seared tuna salade, 74
noodle salad, Thai peanut, 67
nut(s):
  angel hair with walnut pesto, 63
  cherry walnut topping, 57
  endive, apple, and walnut salad, 71
  honey oatmeal bars, 139
  pine, penne with fennel, lemon and, 68
  savory herbed, 52
  Thai peanut noodle salad, 67

oatmeal honey nut bars, 139

Old Farmhouse Chutney, roast beef on rye with, 43

omelet, jelly, 17

orange:

–balsamic vinegar sauce, strawberries in, 147

blood, martini, 151

orzo-basmati pilaf, toasted, swordfish kebabs with, 85

oven-roasted spiced fries, 119

oyster, smoked, topping, 57

pancakes, buttermilk, 19

pan-seared scallops with roasted sweet potatoes, 82–83

pastas, 63–68

angel hair with walnut pesto, 63

baked macaroni and cheese, 65

penne with fennel, lemon, and pine nuts, 68

spicy linguine with shrimp, 64

Thai peanut noodle salad, 67

peach:

coconut sorbet, 131

-mango soup, 32

Melba shortcakes, 141–42

peanut noodle salad, Thai, 67

penne with fennel, lemon, and pine nuts, 68

pesto:

mashed potatoes, 122

walnut, angel hair with, 63

pilaf, toasted basmati-orzo, swordfish kebabs with, 85

pine nuts, penne with fennel, lemon and, 68

pork tenderloins, Moroccan, 111

potato(es):

Bombay salad, 123

oven-roasted spiced fries, 119

pesto mashed, 122

spicy Maine home fries, 14

pot pie, seafood, 86–87

products, Stonewall Kitchen, 156–57

prosciutto, curried, topping, 57

pumpkin-cranberry spice bread, 15

quesadillas, mango-Brie, 48–49

rack of lamb with mustard-herb crust, 110

raspberry cosmopolitan, 154

red pepper–sesame bass, 90–91

rice:

swordfish kebabs with toasted basmati-orzo pilaf, 85

wild, salad with shrimp, 70

roast beef with Old Farmhouse Chutney on rye, 43

roast chicken, Blackberry Sage, 101–2

roasted beets, balsamic, 117

roasted eggplant and smoked mozzarella sandwiches, 38

roasted fennel, sweet and salty, 118

Roasted Garlic & Onion Jam, with smoked turkey on baguette, 42

roasted garlic mayonnaise, 51

cocktail shrimp with, 50

roasted lobster, 79

roasted sweet potatoes, pan-seared scallops with, 82–83

rum, hot apple-buttered, 153

rye, roast beef with Old Farmhouse Chutney on, 43

salads, 63, 69–75

Bombay potato, 123

egg, on black bread, 41

endive, apple, and walnut, 71

lobster tabbouleh, 75

seared tuna niçoise, 74

smoked trout, with cranberry horseradish vinaigrette, 69

Thai peanut noodle, 67

three-color slaw, 126

wild rice with shrimp, 70

salmon:
  sesame-seared, with Lingonberry Jam, 81
  smoked, topping, 57
salsa, sun-dried tomato, 56
sandwiches, 29, 34–43
  egg salad on black bread, 41
  gooey grilled Cheddar-bacon, 34
  roast beef with Old Farmhouse Chutney on rye,
    43
  roasted eggplant and smoked mozzarella, 38
  smoked turkey with Roasted Garlic & Onion Jam
    on baguette, 42
  Southwest shrimp wraps, 39
  Stonewall lobster rolls, 35
satay, shrimp and chicken, with two dipping sauces,
    47
sauces:
  cranberry horseradish vinaigrette, smoked trout
    salad with, 69
  curried mango mayonnaise, 93
  curry-browned butter, fried eggs with chutney
    and, 13
  orange–balsamic vinegar, strawberries in, 147
  roasted garlic mayonnaise, 51
  two dipping, shrimp and chicken satay with, 47
  Vidalia Onion Fig, spareribs with, 107
savory herbed nuts, 52
scallops, pan-seared, with roasted sweet potatoes,
    82–83
scones, spiced, with smoked ham and Cherry
    Chipotle Jam, 59
seafood, 77–95
  pot pie, 86–87
  see also specific seafood
seared tuna salade niçoise, 74
sesame:
  –red pepper bass, 90–91
  -seared salmon with Lingonberry Jam, 81
shortcakes, peach Melba, 141–42

shrimp:
  and chicken satay with two dipping sauces, 47
  cocktail, with roasted garlic mayonnaise, 50
  Southwest wraps, 39
  spicy linguine with, 64
  wild rice salad with, 70
side dishes, 115–27
  balsamic roasted beets, 117
  Bombay potato salad, 123
  green beans with Gorgonzola, 116
  oven-roasted spiced fries, 119
  pesto mashed potatoes, 122
  snow peas and water chestnuts, 127
  sweet and salty roasted fennel, 118
  Swiss chard with bacon and garlic, 124–25
  three-color slaw, 126
slaw, three-color, 126
smoked ham, spiced scones with Cherry Chipotle
    Jam and, 59
smoked mozzarella and roasted eggplant sandwiches, 38
smoked oyster topping, 57
smoked salmon topping, 57
smoked trout salad with cranberry horseradish
    vinaigrette, 69
smoked turkey with Roasted Garlic & Onion Jam
    on baguette, 42
snow peas and water chestnuts, 127
sorbet, coconut peach, 131
soups, 29–33
  corn-crab chowder, 31
  peach-mango, 32
  year-round gazpacho, 33
sour cream blueberry coffee cake, 133–34
Southwest shrimp wraps, 39
spareribs with Vidalia Onion Fig Sauce, 107
spice bread, pumpkin-cranberry, 15
spiced fries, oven-roasted, 119
spiced scones with smoked ham and Cherry
    Chipotle Jam, 59

spicy linguine with shrimp, 64

spicy Maine home fries, 14

spicy white bean dip, 53

steak, flank, fajitas, 105–6

steamed mussels, 95

stir-fried Tomato Ginger chicken, 103

Stonewall Kitchen:

   products, 156–57

   store guide, 155

Stonewall lobster rolls, 35

Stonewall margarita, 152

store guide, Stonewall Kitchen, 155

strawberry(ies):

   lemonade, 150

   in orange–balsamic vinegar sauce, 147

Sunday ham dinner, 112–13

sun-dried tomato salsa, 56

sweet and salty roasted fennel, 118

sweet and savory crostini, 57

sweet potatoes, roasted, pan-seared scallops with,

   82–83

Swiss chard with bacon and garlic, 124–25

swordfish kebabs with toasted basmati-orzo pilaf, 85

tabbouleh lobster salad, 75

tenderloins, Moroccan pork, 111

Thai peanut noodle salad, 67

three-color slaw, 126

thumbprint cookies, 137–38

toasted basmati-orzo pilaf, swordfish kebabs with, 85

tomato, sun-dried, salsa, 56

Tomato Ginger chicken, stir-fried, 103

toppings:

   curried prosciutto, 47

   smoked oyster, 57

   smoked salmon, 57

   walnut cherry, 57

trout, smoked, salad with cranberry horseradish

   vinaigrette, 69

tuna, seared, salade niçoise, 74

turkey, smoked, with Roasted Garlic & Onion Jam

   on baguette, 42

vegetables, 115–27

   balsamic roasted beets, 117

   Bombay potato salad, 123

   green beans with Gorgonzola, 116

   oven-roasted spiced fries, 119

   pesto mashed potatoes, 122

   snow peas and water chestnuts, 127

   sweet and salty roasted fennel, 118

   Swiss chard with bacon and garlic, 124–25

   three-color slaw, 126

Vidalia Onion Fig Sauce, spareribs with, 107

vinaigrette, cranberry horseradish, smoked trout

   salad with, 69

vinegar sauce, orange-balsamic, strawberries in,

   147

walnut:

   cherry topping, 57

   endive, and apple salad, 71

   pesto, angel hair with, 63

water chestnuts and snow peas, 127

white bean dip, spicy, 53

wild rice salad with shrimp, 70

wraps, Southwest shrimp, 39

year-round gazpacho, 33